ONLINE INSTRUCTOR

NX 9 Tutorial

Table of Contents

Introduction

NX as a topic of learning is vast, and having a wide scope. It is one of the world's most advanced and highly integrated CAD/CAM/CAE product. NX delivers a great value to enterprises of all sizes by covering the entire range of product development. It speeds up the design process by simplifying complex product designs.

This tutorial book provides a systematic approach for users to learn NX 9. It is aimed for those with no previous experience with NX. However, users of previous versions of NX may also find this book useful for them to learn the new enhancements. The user will be guided from starting a NX 9 session to constructing parts, assemblies, and drawings. Each chapter has components explained with the help of various dialogs and screen images.

Scope of this Book

This book is written for students and engineers who are interested to learn NX 9 for designing mechanical components and assemblies, and then generate drawings.

This book provides a systematic approach for learning NX 9. The topics include Getting Started with NX 9, Basic Part Modeling, Constructing Assemblies, Constructing Drawings, Additional Modeling Tools, and Sheet Metal Modeling.

Chapter 1 introduces NX 9. The user interface, terminology, mouse functions, and shortcut keys are discussed in this chapter.

Chapter 2 takes you through the creation of your first NX model. You construct simple parts.

Chapter 3 teaches you to construct assemblies. It explains the Top-down and Bottom-up approaches for designing an assembly. You construct an assembly using the Bottom-up approach.

Chapter 4 teaches you to generate drawings of the models constructed in the earlier chapters. You will also learn to generate exploded views, and part list of an assembly.

Chapter 5: In this chapter, you will learn additional modeling tools to construct complex models.

Chapter 6 introduces you to NX Sheet Metal design. You will construct a sheet metal part using the tools available in the NX Sheet Metal environment.

Chapter 1: Getting Started

In this chapter, you will learn some of the most commonly used features of NX. Also, you will learn about the user interface.

In NX, you construct 3D parts and use them to create 2D drawings and 3D assemblies.

NX is Feature Based. Features are shapes that are combined to build a part. You can modify these shapes individually.

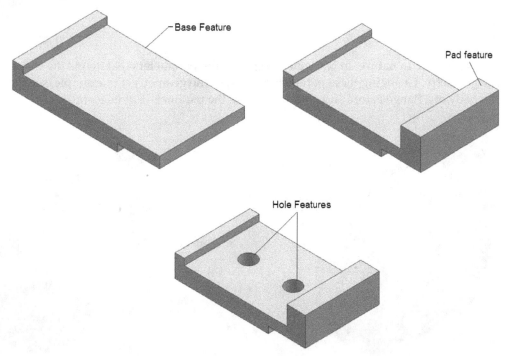

Most of the features are sketch-based. A sketch is a 2D profile and can be extruded, revolved, or swept along a path to construct features.

NX 9 Tutorial

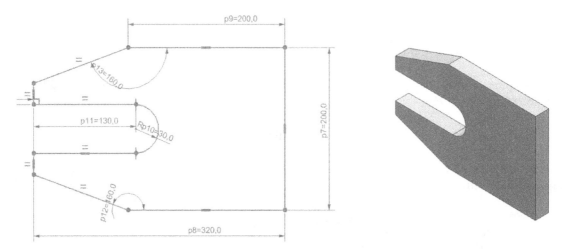

NX is parametric in nature. In NX, you can specify the parameters that define the shape and size of the geometry. Changing these parameters changes the geometry. For example, see the design of the body of a flange before and after modifying the parameters of its features.

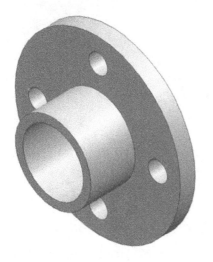

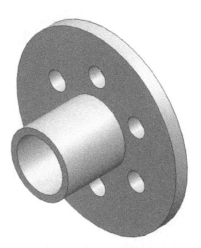

Starting NX

1. Click the **Start** button on the Windows taskbar.

2. Click **All Programs**.

3. Click **Siemens NX 9.0**.

NX 9 Tutorial

4. Click **NX 9**.

5. Click the **New** button.

6. On the **New** dialog, click **Templates > Model**.

7. Click the **OK** button

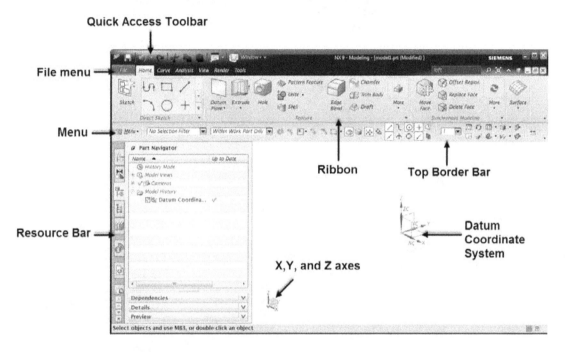

Notice these important features of the NX window.

User Interface

Various components of the user interface are:

Quick Access Toolbar

This is located on the top left corner. It has some commonly used commands such as **Save, Undo, Redo, Copy,** and so on.

NX 9 Tutorial

File Menu

The **File Menu** appears when you click on the **File** icon located at the top left corner of the window. The **File Menu** has a list of self-explanatory menus. You can see a list of recently opened documents under the **Recently Opened Parts** section. You can also switch to different applications of NX.

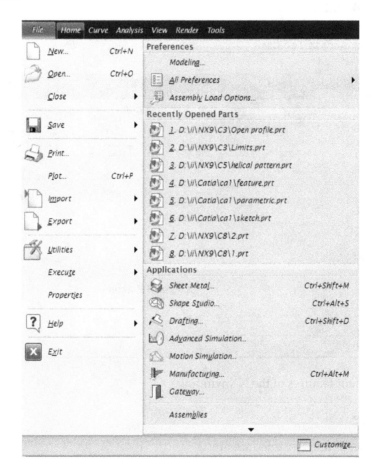

Ribbon

A ribbon is a set of tools, which help you perform various operations. It has tabs and groups. Various tabs of the ribbon are:

Home tab
This ribbon tab contains the tools such as **New**, **Open**, **Help**, and so on.

NX 9 Tutorial

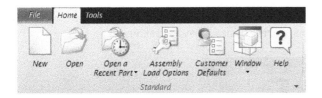

Home tab in the Model template
This ribbon tab has the tools to construct 3D features.

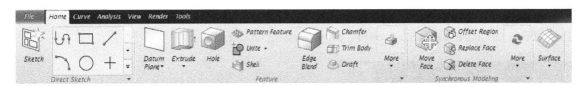

View tab
This ribbon tab has the tools to modify the display of the model and user interface.

Analysis tab
This ribbon tab has the tools to measure objects. It also has tools to analyze the draft, curvature, and surface of the model geometry.

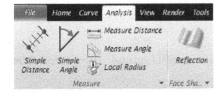

Home tab in Sketch Task environment
This ribbon tab has all the sketch tools. It is available in a separate environment called Sketch Task environment.

NX 9 Tutorial

Tools tab

This ribbon tab has the tools to create expressions, part families, movies, fasteners.

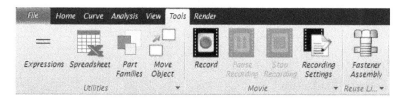

Render tab

This ribbon tab has the tools to generate photorealistic images.

Assemblies group

This group contains the tools to construct an assembly.

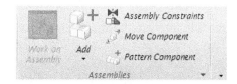

Drafting template ribbon

In the Drafting template, you can generate orthographic views of the 3D model. The ribbon tabs in this environment contain tools to generate 2D drawings.

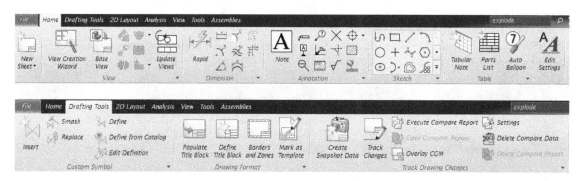

NX 9 Tutorial

Sheet Metal ribbon

The tools in this ribbon help you to construct sheet metal components.

Some tabs are not visible by default. To display a particular tab, right-click on the ribbon and select it from the list displayed.

You can also add a ribbon tab by opening the **Customize** dialog.

NX 9 Tutorial

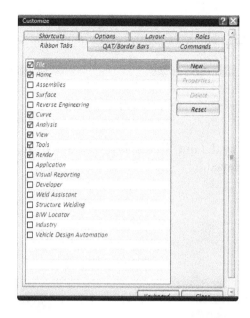

Ribbon Groups and More Galleries

The tools on the ribbon are arranged in various groups depending upon their use. Each group has a **More Gallery**, which contains additional tools.

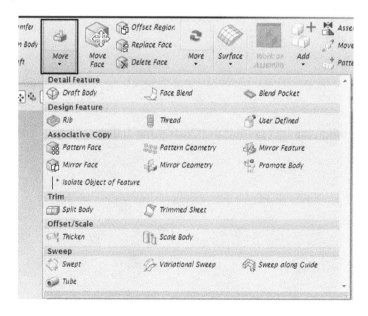

NX 9 Tutorial

You can add more tools to a ribbon group by clicking the arrow located at the bottom right corner of a group.

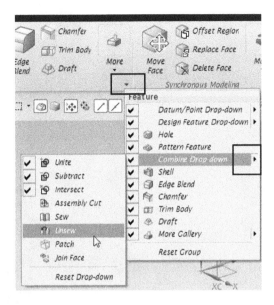

Top Border Bar

This is available below the ribbon. It has all the options to filter the objects that you can select from the graphics window.

Menu
Menu is located on the Top Border Bar. It has various options (menu titles). When you click on a menu title, a drop-down appears. Select any option from this drop-down.

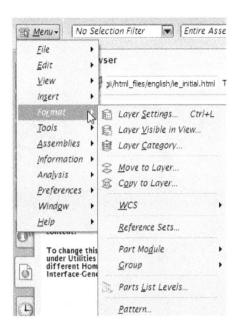

Status bar

This is available below the graphics window. It shows the prompts and the action taken while using the tools.

Select planar face to sketch or select section geometry | Single Curve : Edge of Extrude(1)

Resource Bar

This is located on the left side. It has all the navigator windows such as Assembly Navigator, Constraint Navigator, Part Navigator, and so on.

Part Navigator

Contains the list of operations carried while constructing a part.

NX 9 Tutorial

Roles Navigator

The **Roles** Navigator has a list of system default and industry specific roles. A role is a set of tools and ribbon tabs customized for a specific application. For example, the **CAM Express** role can be used for performing manufacturing operations. This textbook uses the **Essentials** role.

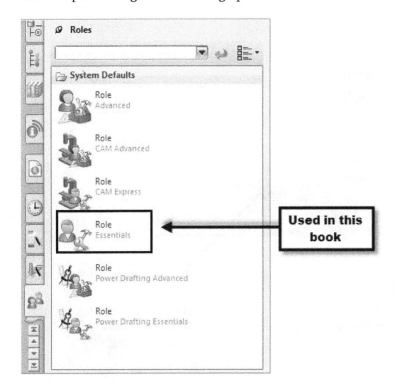

NX 9 Tutorial

Dialogs

When you execute any command in NX, the dialog related to it appears. A dialog has of various options. The following figure shows various components of a dialog.

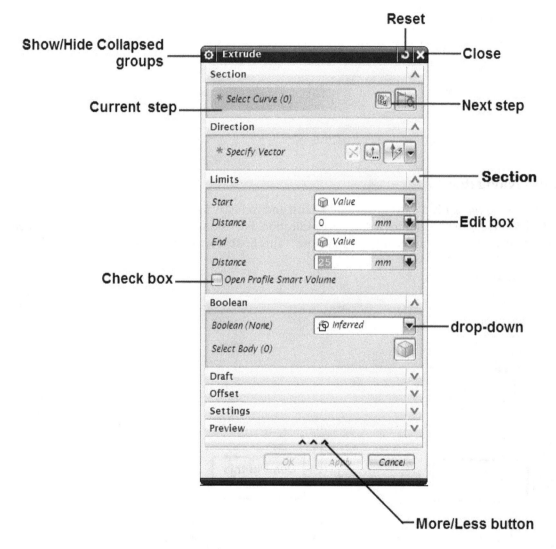

This textbook uses the default options on the dialog. If you have made any changes on a dialog, click the **Reset** button on the dialog; the default options appear.

NX 9 Tutorial

Mouse Functions

Various functions of the mouse buttons are:

Left Mouse button (MB1)
When you double-click the left mouse button (MB1) on an object, the dialog related to the object appears. Using this dialog, you can edit the parameters of the objects.

Middle Mouse button (MB2)
Click this button to execute the **OK** command.

Right Mouse button (MB3)
Click this button to open the shortcut menu.

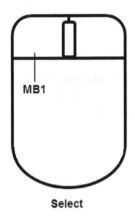

Select

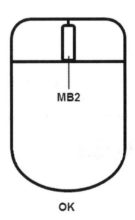

OK

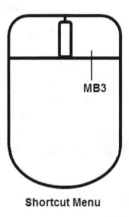

Shortcut Menu

The other functions with combination of the three mouse buttons are:

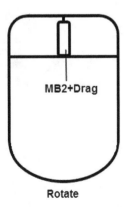

Rotate

Zoom In/Out

Pan

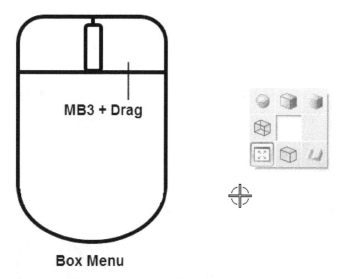

Box Menu

Color Settings

To change the background color of the window, click **Menu > Preferences > Background**. On the **Edit Background** dialog, click the **Plain** option to change the background to plain. Click on the color swatches. On the **Color** dialog, change the background color and click **OK** twice.

NX 9 Tutorial

Shortcut Keys

CTRL+Z	(Undo)
CTRL+Y	(Repeat)
CTRL+S	(Save)
F5	(Refresh)
F1	(NX Help)
F6	(Zoom)
F7	(Rotate)
CTRL+M	(Starts the Modeling environment)
CTRL+SHIFT+D	(Starts the Drafting environment)
CTRL+ALT+N	(Starts the NX Sheet Metal environment)
CTRL+ALT+M	(Starts the Manufacturing environment)
X	(Extrude)
CTRL+1	(Customize)
CTRL+D	(Delete)
CTRL+N	(New File)
CTRL+O	(Open File)
CTRL+P	(Plot)

Chapter 2: Modeling Basics

This chapter takes you through the creation of your first NX model. You construct simple parts:

In this chapter, you will:

- Construct Sketches
- Construct a base feature
- Add another feature to it
- Construct revolved features
- Construct Blocks
- Apply draft

TUTORIAL 1

This tutorial takes you through the creation of your first NX model. You construct the Disc of an Old ham coupling:

Starting a New Part File

1. To start a new part, click the **New** button on ribbon.

2. On the **New** dialog, the **Model** template

is the default selection. Therefore, click **OK** to open new model window.

Starting a Sketch

1. To start a new sketch, click **Home > Direct Sketch > Sketch** on the ribbon.

NX 9 Tutorial

2. Select the XZ plane.

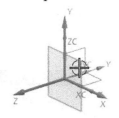

3. Click the **OK** button to start the sketch.

The first feature is extruded from a sketched circular profile. You will begin by sketching the circle.

4. On the ribbon, click **Home > Direct Sketch > Circle**.

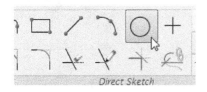

Direct Sketch

5. Click on the sketch origin.

6. Drag the cursor and click to draw a circle

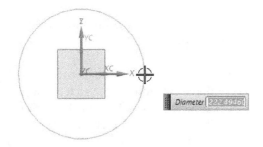

7. Press **ESC** to deactivate the tool.

Adding Dimensions

In this section, you will define the size of the sketched circle by adding dimensions.

Note: You may notice that dimensions are applied automatically. However, they do not constraint the sketch.

As you add dimensions, the sketch can attain any one of the following three states:

Fully Constrained sketch: In a fully constrained sketch, the positions of all the entities are fully described by dimensions, constraints, or both. In a fully constrained sketch, all the entities are dark green color.

Under Constrained sketch: Additional dimensions, constraints, or both are needed to completely define the geometry. In this state, you can drag the sketch elements to modify the sketch. An under constrained sketch element is in maroon color.

Over Constrained sketch: In this state, an object has conflicting dimensions, constraints, or both. An over constrained sketch element is red. The effected entities are in magenta color.

1. Double-click on the sketch dimension.

2. In the **Dimension** box, type-in 100, and then press **Enter**.

3. Press **Esc** to deactivate the **Rapid Dimension** tool.

To display the entire circle at a full size and to center it in the graphics window, use one of the following methods:

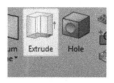

- Click **Fit** on **Top Border Bar**.
- On the ribbon, click **View > Orientation > Fit**.

4. On the ribbon, click **Home > Direct Sketch > Finish Sketch**.

5. To change the view to isometric, click **Orient View** drop-down **> Isometric** on the **Top Border Bar**.

You can use the buttons on the **Orient View** Drop-down on the **Top Border Bar** to set the view orientation of the sketch, part, or assembly.

Constructing the Base Feature
The first feature in any part is called the base feature. You construct this feature by extruding the sketched circle.

1. On the ribbon, click **Home > Feature > Extrude**.

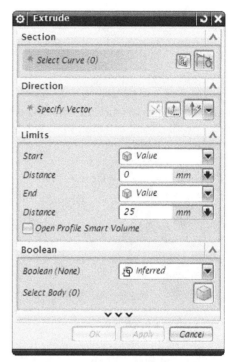

2. Click on the sketch.

3. Type-in 10 in the **End** box attached to the preview.

4. To see how the model would look if you have extruded the sketch in the opposite direction, click **Reverse Direction** button in the **Direction** section. Again, click on it to extrude the sketch in the front direction.

5. Under the **Settings** section, select **Body Type > Solid**.

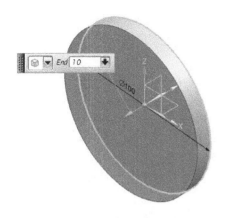

6. Click **OK** to construct the extrusion.

Notice the new feature, **Extrude**, in the **Part Navigator**.

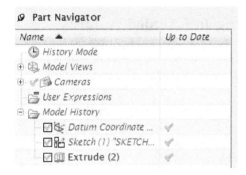

To magnify a model in the graphics window, you can use the **Orientation** tools on the **View** tab.

Click **Fit** to display the part full size in the current window.

Click **Zoom**, and then drag the pointer to draw a rectangle; the area in the rectangle zooms to fill the window.

Click **Zoom In/Out**, and then drag the pointer. Dragging up zooms out; dragging down zooms in.

Click a vertex, an edge, or a feature, and then click **Fit View to Selection**; the selected item zooms to fill the window.

To display the part in different modes, click the buttons on the **Style** group on the **View** tab.

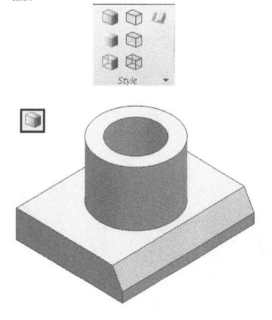

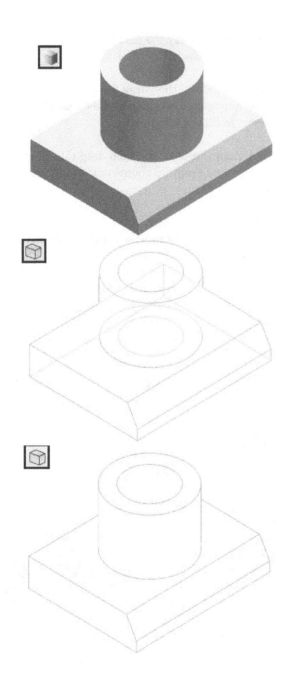

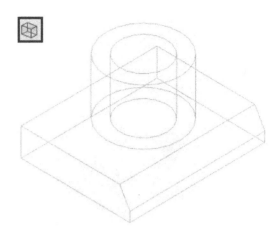

The default display mode for parts and assemblies is **Shaded with Edges**. You may change the display mode whenever you want.

Adding an Extruded Feature

To construct additional features on the part, you need to sketch on the model faces or planes, and then extrude the sketches.

1. Click **Static Wireframe** on the **View** tab.

2. On the ribbon, click **Home > Direct Sketch > Sketch**.

3. Click on the front face of the part to select it, and then click **OK**.

4. On the ribbon, click **Direct sketch > More Curve > Project Curve**.

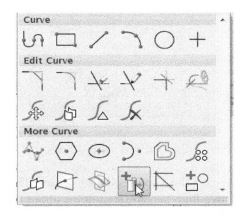

5. Click on the circular edge.

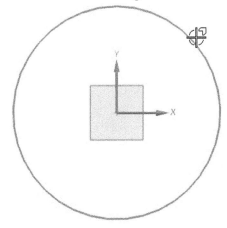

6. On the **Project Curve** dialog, click **OK** to project the circular edge onto the sketch plane.

7. Click **Line** on the **Direct Sketch** group.

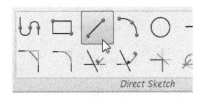

8. Click on the circle to define the first point of the line.

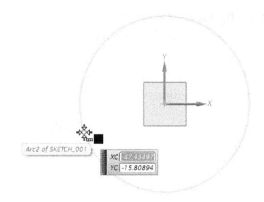

9. Drag the cursor towards right.

10. Click on the circle to draw a line.

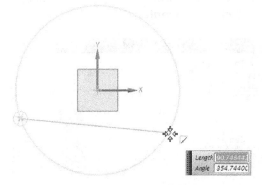

11. Draw another line above the previous line.

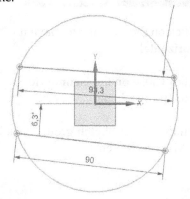

Adding Constraints and Dimensions to the Sketch

To establish the location and size of the sketch, you have to add the necessary constraints and dimensions.

1. Click **Geometric Constraints** on the **Direct Sketch** group.

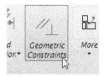

2. On the **Geometric Constraints** dialog, click **Horizontal**.

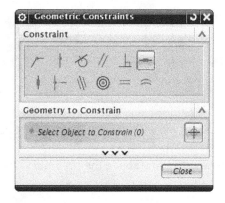

3. Click on the first line to make it horizontal.

4. Click **Close** on the **Geometric Constraint** dialog.

5. On the **Direct Sketch** group, click **More > Make Symmetric**.

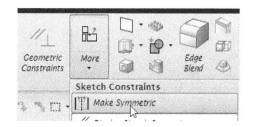

6. Select the first and second lines.

7. Select the X-axis as the centerline. The two lines become symmetric about the X-axis.

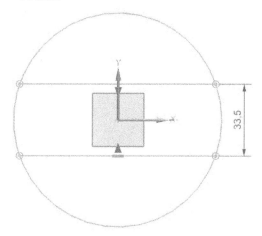

8. On the **Make Symmetric** dialog, click **Close**.

Adding Dimensions

9. Double-click on the sketch dimension.

10. Type-in 12 in the box displayed.

11. Click **Close** on the dialog.

Trimming Sketch Entities

1. Click **Trim Recipe Curve** on the **Direct Sketch** group.

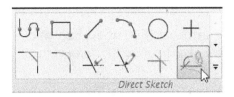

Direct Sketch

2. Click on the projected element.

3. Click on the two horizontal lines.

4. On the **Trim Recipe Curve** dialog, click **Discard** under the **Region** section.

5. Click **OK** to trim the projected elements.

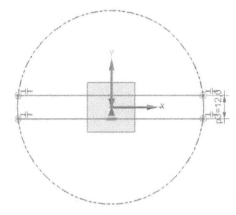

6. Click **Finish Sketch** on the **Direct Sketch** group.

7. To change the view to isometric, click **View > Orientation > Isometric** on the ribbon.

Extruding the Sketch

1. Click on the sketch, and then click **Extrude** on the **Contextual** toolbar.

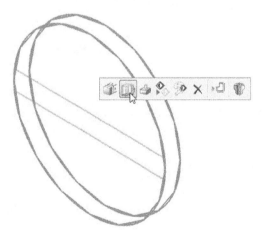

2. Type-in 10 in the **End** box attached to the preview.

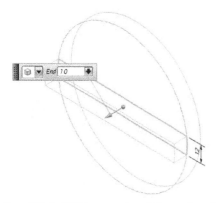

3. Click **OK** to construct the extrusion.

4. To hide the sketch, click **View> Show and Hide** on the ribbon.

5. On the **Show and Hide** dialog, click **Hide Sketches** to hide the sketches.

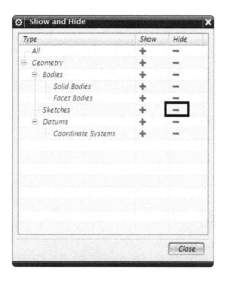

6. Click **Close**.

Adding another Extruded Feature

1. Draw a sketch on the back face of the base feature.

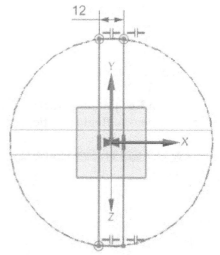

You can use the **Rotate** button on the **View** group to rotate the model.

2. Click **Finish Sketch** on the ribbon.

3. Extrude the sketch with 10 mm thickness.

4. Press F7 and rotate the model

To move the part view, click **View > Orientation > Pan**, then drag the mouse to move the part around in the graphics window.

5. On the ribbon, click **View > Style > Shaded with Edges**.

Saving the Part

1. Click **Save** on the **Quick Access Toolbar**.

2. On the **Name Parts** dialog, type-in **Disc** in the **Name** box and click the **Folder** button.

3. Browse to the NX 9/C2 folder, and then click **OK** twice.

4. Click **File > Close > All parts**.

Note:
*.prt is the file extension for all the files constructed in the Modeling, Assembly, and Drafting environments of NX.

TUTORIAL 2

In this tutorial, you construct a flange by performing the following:

-   Constructing a revolved feature
-   Constructing a cut features

-   Adding fillets

Open a New Part File

1. To open a new part, click **File > New** on the ribbon.

2. On the **New** dialog, the **Model** is the default selection. So click **OK** to open a new model window.

Sketching a Revolve Profile

You construct the base feature of the flange by revolving a profile around a centerline.

1. Click the **Sketch** button on the **Direct Sketch** group.

2. Select the YZ plane.

3. Click the **OK** button to start the sketch.

4. Click **Profile** on the **Direct Sketch** group.

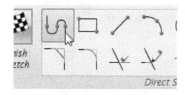

5. Draw a sketch similar to that shown in figure.

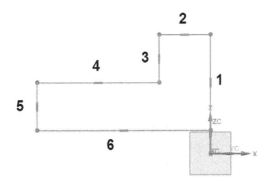

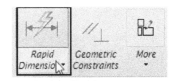

6.   Click **Geometric Constraints** on the **Direct Sketch** group.

7.   On the **Geometric Constraints** dialog, click **Collinear**.

8.   Expand the **Geometric Constraints** dialog by clicking the three arrows at the bottom.

9.   Under the **Settings** section, check **Automatic Selection Progression**.

10. Click on the line 1 and the Y-axis to make them collinear.

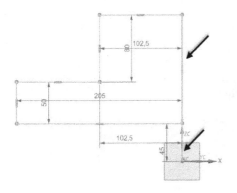

11. Click **Rapid Dimension** on the **Direct Sketch** group.

12. Select the X-axis and Line 6; a dimension appears.

13. Place the dimension and type-in 15 in the dimension box.

14. Press **Enter**.

15. Click on the X-axis and Line 4; a dimension appears.

16. Set the dimension to 30 mm.

17. Click on the X-axis and Line 2; a dimension appears.

18. Set the dimension to 50 mm.

19. Create a dimension between the Y-axis and Line 3.

20. Set the dimension to 20 mm.

21. Create a dimension of 50 mm between Y-axis and Line 5.

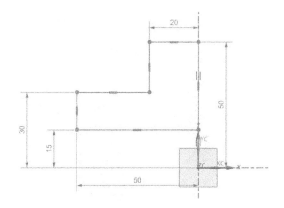

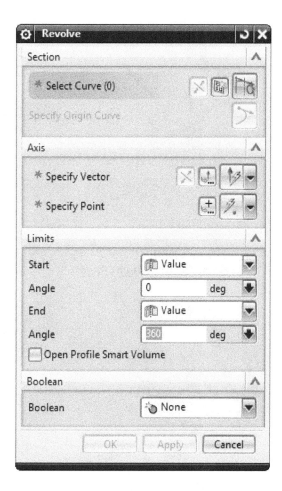

22. Click **Finish Sketch** on the **Direct Sketch** group.

23. To change the view to isometric, click **View > Orientation > Isometric** on the ribbon.

Constructing the Revolved Feature

1. On the ribbon, click **Home > Feature > Extrude > Revolve.**

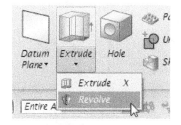

2. Click on the sketch.

3. Under the **Axis** section, click **Specify Vector**.

4. On the vector triad, click the Y-axis.

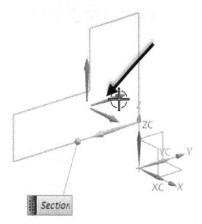

5. Click on the origin point. The preview of the revolved feature appears.

Constructing the Cut feature

1. Click **Extrude** on the **Feature** group.

2. Rotate the model geometry and click on the back face of the part.

3. Construct a sketch, as shown in figure.

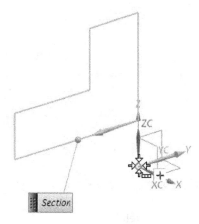

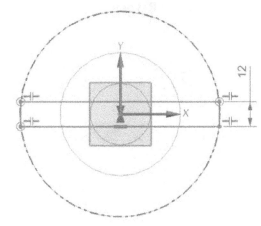

6. Type-in 360 in the **End** box.

7. Click **OK** to construct the revolved feature.

4. Click **Finish** on the **Sketch** group.

5. Enter 10 in the **End** box attached to the preview.

6. Under the **Direction** section, click

Reverse Direction.

7. Under the **Boolean** section, select **Subtract**.

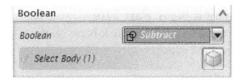

8. Click **OK** to construct the cut feature.

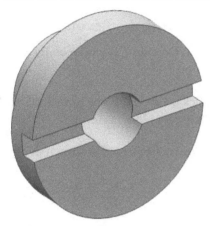

Adding another Cutout

1. Draw sketch on the front face of the model geometry.

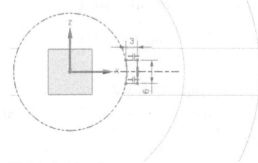

2. Finish the sketch.

3. Orient the model to Isometric.

4. Click **Extrude** on the **Feature** group.

5. Click on the sketch.

6. On the **Extrude** dialog, under the **Limits** section, select **End > Through All**.

7. Under the **Direction** section, click **Reverse Direction**.

8. Under the **Boolean** section, select **Subtract**.

9. Click **OK** to construct the cutout feature.

Adding the Edge blend

1. Click **Home > Feature > Edge Blend** on the ribbon.

2. Click on the inner circular edge and set **Radius 1** to 5.

3. Click **OK** to add the blend.

Saving the Part

1. Click **File > Save > Save**.

2. On the **Name Parts** dialog, type **Flange** in the **Name** box.

3. Click **OK**.

4. Click **File > Close > All Parts**.

TUTORIAL 3

In this tutorial, you construct a Shaft by

performing the following:

- Constructing a revolved feature
- Constructing a cut feature

Opening a New Part File

1. To open a new part, click **New** on the **Standard** group.

2. Select the **Model** template and click **OK**; a new model window appears.

Constructing the Revolved Feature

1. Click **Extrude > Revolve** on the **Feature** group.

2. Click on the YZ plane to select it, and then click **OK**.

3. Construct a sketch, as shown in figure.

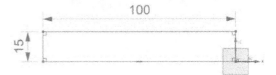

4. Click **Finish** on the **Sketch** group.

5. Click on the Y-axis of the triad.

6. Click on the origin point.

7. Click **OK** to construct the revolved feature.

Creating Cut feature

1. Construct a sketch on the front face of the model geometry.

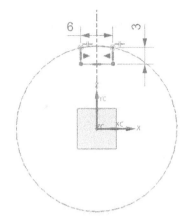

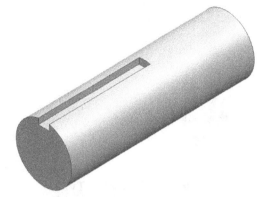

2. Finish the sketch.

3. Orient the model to Isometric.

4. Click **Extrude** on the **Feature** group.

5. Click on the sketch.

6. Type-in 55 in the **End** box.

7. Under the **Direction** section, click the **Reverse Direction** button.

8. Under the **Boolean** section, select **Subtract**.

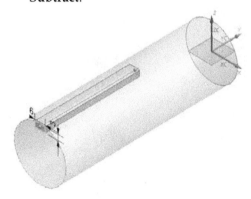

9. Click **OK** to construct the cut feature.

Saving the Part

1. Click **File > Save > Save**;

2. On the **Name Parts** dialog, type **Shaft** in the **Name** box.

3. Click **OK**.

4. Click **File > Close > All Parts**.

TUTORIAL 4

In this tutorial, you construct a Key by performing the following:

- Constructing a Block
- Applying draft

Constructing Extruded feature

1. Open a new part file.

2. On the ribbon, click **Home > Feature > More > Design Feature > Block**.

31

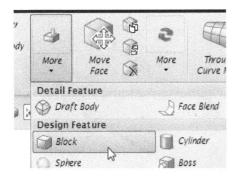

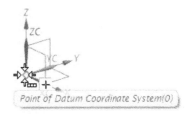

3. On the **Block** dialog, select **Type > Origin and Edge Lengths**.

4. Type-in **6**, **50**, and **6** in the **Length (XC)**, **Width (YC)**, and **Height (ZC)** boxes, respectively.

6. Click **OK** to construct the block.

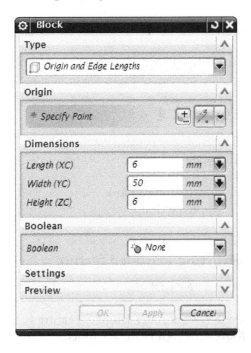

Applying Draft

1. Click **Draft** on the **Feature** group.

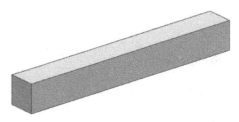

2. On the **Draft** dialog, select **Type > From Plane or Surface**.

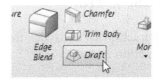

5. Click on the origin point of the datum coordinate system.

3. Click on Y-axis to specify vector.

4. Select the front face as the stationary face.

5. Under the **Faces to Draft** section, click **Select Face**.

6. Select the top face.

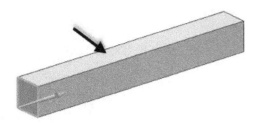

7. Type-in 1 in the **Angle 1** box.

8. Click **OK** to add the draft.

Saving the Part

1. Click **File > Save > Save.**

2. On the **Name Parts** dialog, type **Key** in the **Name** box.

3. Click **OK.**

4. Click **File > Close > All Parts**.

Chapter 3: Constructing Assembly

In this chapter, you will:

- Add Components to an assembly
- Apply constraints between components
- Produce exploded view of the assembly

TUTORIAL 1

This tutorial takes you through the creation of your first assembly. You construct the Oldham coupling assembly:

Copying the Part files into a new folder

1. Create a folder named **Oldham_Coupling** at the location NX 9/C3.

2. Copy all the part files constructed in the previous chapter to this folder.

Opening a New Assembly File

1. To open a new assembly, click **File > New**.

2. On the **New** dialog, click **Assembly** in the **Template** section.

3. Click **OK** to open a new assembly window.

Inserting the Base Component

1. On the **Add Component** dialog, under the **Part** section, click **Open** button.

2. Browse to the location NX 9/C3/Oldham_Coupling and double-click on **Flange.prt**.

3. On the **Add Component** dialog, under the **Placement** section, select **Positioning > Absolute Origin**.

4. Under the **Settings** section, select **Reference Set > Entire Part**.

5. Click **OK** to place the Flange at the origin.

There are two ways of constructing any assembly model.

- Top-Down Approach
- Bottom-Up Approach

Top-Down Approach
You open the assembly file, and then construct components files in it.

Bottom-Up Approach
You construct the components first, and then add them to the assembly file. In this tutorial, you construct the assembly using this approach.

Adding the second component

1. To insert the second component, click **Assemblies > Component > Add** on the ribbon.

2. On the **Add Component** dialog, under the **Part** section, click the **Open** button.

3. Browse to the location NX 9/C3/Oldham_Coupling, and then double-click on **Shaft.prt**.

4. Under the **Placement** section, select **Positioning > By Constraints**.

5. Under the **Settings** section, select **Reference Set > Entire Part**.

6. Click **OK** on the **Add Component** dialog.

After adding the components to the assembly environment, you have to apply constraints between them. By applying constraints, you establish relationships between components. You can apply the following types of constraints between components.

Touch Align: Using this constraint, you can make two faces coplanar to each other. Note that if you set the **Orientation** to **Align**, the faces will point in the same direction. You can also align the centerlines of the cylindrical faces.

Concentric: This constraint makes the centers of circular edges coincident. In addition, the circular edges will be on the same plane.

Distance: This constraint provides an offset distance between two objects.

Fix: This constraint fixes a component at its current position.

Parallel: This constraint makes two objects parallel to each other.

Perpendicular: This constraint makes two objects perpendicular to each other.

Fit: This constraint brings two cylindrical faces together. Note that they should have the same radius.

Bond: This constraint makes the selected components rigid so that they move together.

Center: This constraint positions the selected component at a center plane between two components.

Angle: Applies angle between two components.

Align/Lock: Aligns the axes of two cylindrical faces and locks the rotation.

7. On the **Assembly Constraints** dialog, select **Type > Touch Align**.

8. Under the **Geometry to Constrain**

section, select **Orientation > Infer Center/Axis**.

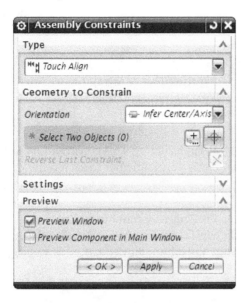

9. Click on the cylindrical face of the Shaft.

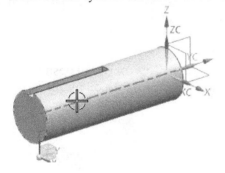

10. Click on the inner cylindrical face of the Flange.

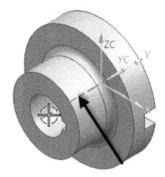

11. Under the **Geometry to Constrain** section, select **Orientation > Align**.

12. Click on the front face of the shaft.

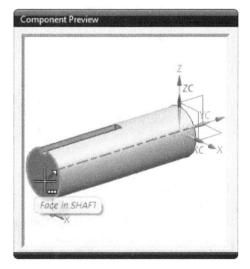

13. Press F7 and rotate the flange to view its backside.

14. Press F7 again to deactivate the **Rotate** tool.

15. Click on the slot face, as shown in figure.

NX 9 Tutorial

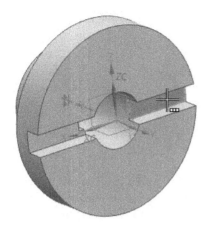

16. Click on the YZ plane of the Shaft.

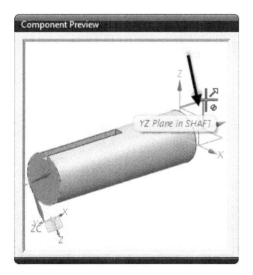

17. Click on the XY plane of the Flange.

18. Click **OK** to assemble the components.

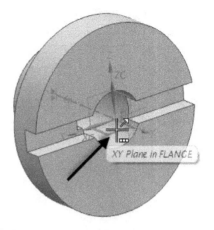

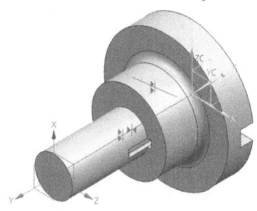

Checking the Degrees of the Freedom

1. To check the degrees of freedom of a component, click **Assemblies > Component Position > Show Degrees of Freedom** on the ribbon.

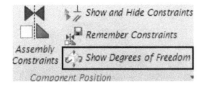

2. Click on the Flange to display the degrees of freedom.

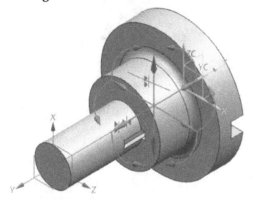

You will notice that the Flange has six degrees of freedom.

Fixing the Flange

1. To fix the flange, click **Assemblies > Component Position > Assembly Constraints** on the ribbon.

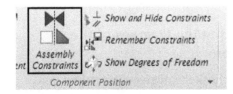

2. On the **Assembly Constraints** dialog, click **Type > Fix**.

3. Click on the Flange, and then click **OK**.

4. On the ribbon, click **View > Orientation > More > Refresh**.

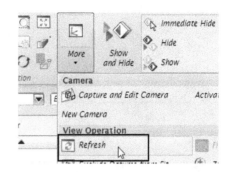

5. To view the degrees of freedom, click **Show Degrees of Freedom** on the **Component Position** group and select the Flange and Shaft.

You will notice that they are fully constrained.

Hiding the Flange

1. To hide the Flange, click on it and select **Hide** from the contextual toolbar.

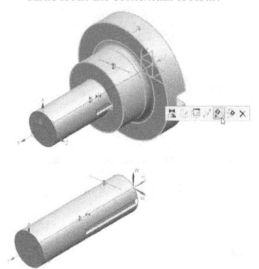

Adding the Third Component

1. Click **Add** on the **Component** group.

2. On the **Add Component** dialog, click the **Open** button.

3. Double-click on the **Key.prt**.

4. Click **OK**.

5. On the **Assembly Constraints** dialog, select **Type > Touch Align**.

6. Under the **Geometry to Constraints** section, select **Orientation > Align**.

7. Click on the front face of the Key and front face of the Shaft.

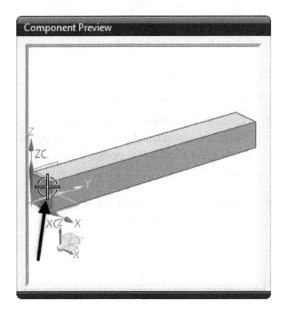

8. Click on the XY plane of the Key.

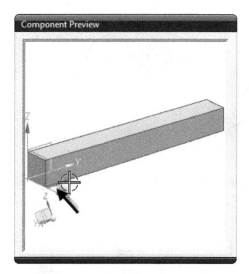

9. Click on the face on the shaft, as shown in figure.

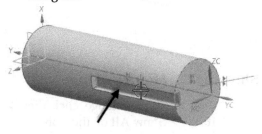

10. Under the **Geometry to Constrain** section, select **Orientation > Touch**.

11. Click on the side face of the Key and select the face on shaft, as shown in figure.

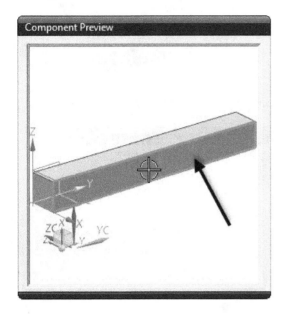

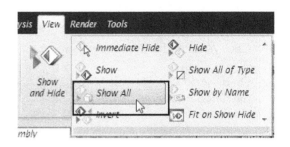

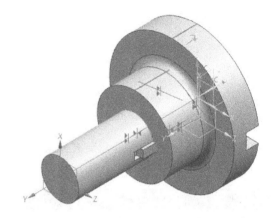

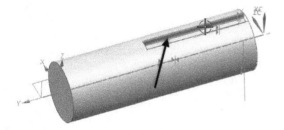

Hiding the Reference Planes, sketches, and Constraint symbols

1. To hide the reference planes and sketches, open the **Assembly Navigator** and select all the components of the assembly.

12. Click **OK**.

Showing the Hidden Flange

1. To show the hidden flange, click **View > Visibility > Show All** on the ribbon.

2. Click the right mouse button and select **Replace Reference Set > MODEL**.

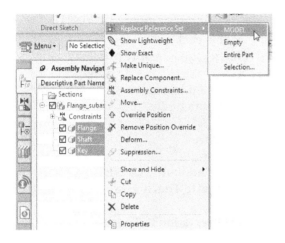

3. To hide the constraint symbols, click the right mouse button on **Constraints** and uncheck **Display Constraints in Graphics Window**.

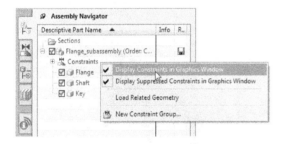

Saving the Assembly

1. Click **File > Save > Save**.

2. On the **Name Parts** dialog, type-in **Flange_subassembly** in the **Name** box and click the **Folder** button.

3. Browse to NX 9/C3/Oldham_Coupling folder, and then click **OK** twice.

4. Click **File > Close > All Parts**.

Starting the Main assembly

1. Click **File > New**.

2. On the **New** dialog, click the **Assembly** template.

3. Type-in **Main_assembly** in the **Name** box and click the **Folder** button.

4. Browse to NX 9/C3/ Oldham_Coupling folder, and then click **OK** twice.

Adding Disc to the Assembly

1. On the **Add Components** dialog, click

the **Open** button.

2. Double-click on **Disc.prt**.

3. Under the **Placement** section, select
   Positioning > Absolute Origin.

4. Set **Reference Set** to **Model**
   ("MODEL").

5. Click **OK** to place the Disc at the origin.

Fixing the Disc to the Origin

1. Click **Assemblies > Component
   Position > Assembly Constraints** on the
   ribbon.

2. On the **Assembly Constraints** dialog,
   select **Type > Fix**.

3. Select the Disc and click **OK**.

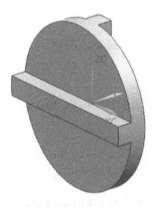

Placing the Sub-assembly

1. Click **Add** button on the **Component**
   group.

2. Click the **Open** button.

3. Double-click on
   Flange_subassembly.prt.

4. On the **Add Component** dialog, select
   Positioning > By Constraints.

5. Click **OK**.

6. On the **Assembly Constraints** dialog,
   set **Type** to **Touch Align**

7. Set **Orientation** to **Touch**.

8. Click on the face on the Flange, as
   shown in figure.

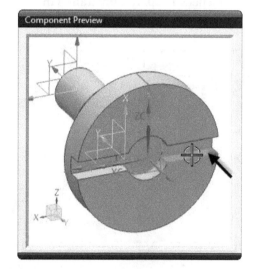

9. Click on the face on the Disc, as shown
   in figure.

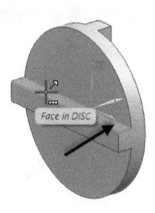

10. On the **Assembly Constraints** dialog, set **Type** to **Concentric.**

11. Click on the circular edge of the Flange.

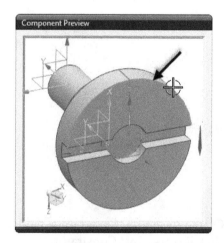

12. Click on the circular edge of the Disc.

13. Click **OK** to assemble the subassembly.

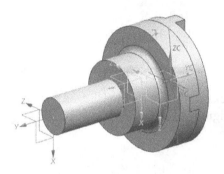

Assembling second instance of the Sub-assembly

1. Insert another instance of the Flange subassembly.

2. On the **Assembly Constraints** dialog, set **Type** to **Touch Align**

3. Set **Orientation** to **Touch**.

4. Click on the face on the Flange, as shown in figure

NX 9 Tutorial

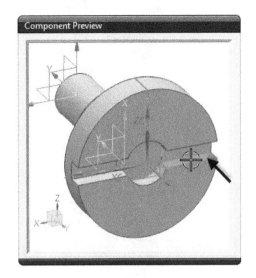

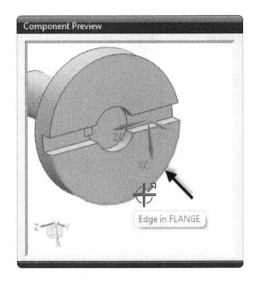

5. Click on the face on the Disc, as shown in figure.

8. Click on the circular edge of the Disc.

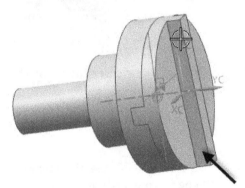

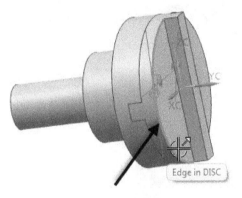

6. On the **Assembly Constraints** dialog, set **Type** to **Concentric.**

7. Click on the circular edge of the Flange.

9. On the **Assembly Constraints** dialog, click **Reverse Last Constraint**.

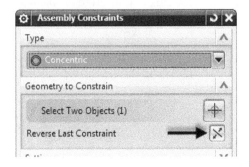

46

10. Click **OK**.

Saving the Assembly

1. Click **Save** on the **Quick Access Toolbar**, or click **File > Save**

TUTORIAL 2

In this tutorial, you produce the exploded view of the assembly created in the previous tutorial:

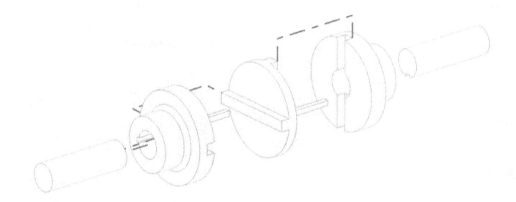

Producing the Exploded view

1. To produce the exploded view, click
   Exploded Views > New Explosion.

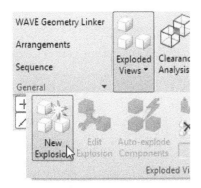

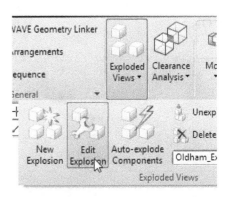

2. On the **New Explosion** dialog, type-in **Oldham_Explosion** in the **Name** box.

3. Click **OK**.

4. On the **Assembly Navigator**, click the right mouse button on Flange_subassembly x 2.

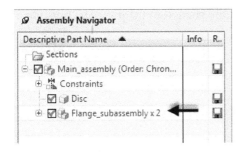

5. Select **Unpack**.

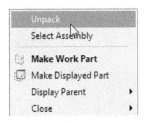

6. Click **Exploded Views > Edit Explosion** on the ribbon.

7. Select Flange_subassembly from the **Assembly Navigator**.

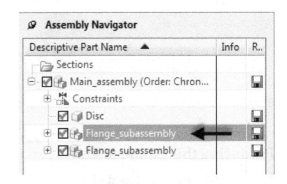

8. Click **Move Objects** on the dialog. The

dynamic CSYS appears on the flange subassembly.

9. Click the **Snap Handles to WCS** button on the **Edit Explosion** dialog; the dynamic CSYS snaps to WCS.

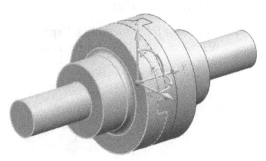

10. Click the **Y-Handle** on the dynamic CSYS.

11. Enter **-100** in the **Distance** box.

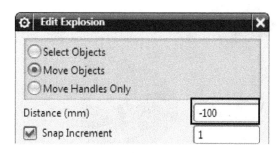

12. Click **OK** to explode the flange subassembly.

13. Click the **Edit Explosion** button on the **Exploded Views** group.

14. On the **Edit Explosion** dialog, click **Select Objects**.

15. Rotate the model and select the Key from the assembly.

16. Click **Move Objects** on the dialog.

17. Click the **Snap Handles to WCS** button.

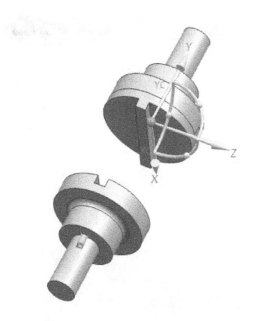

23. Likewise, explode the other flange subassembly and its parts in the opposite direction. The explosion distances are same.

18. Click the **Y-Handle** on the dynamic CSYS.

19. Enter **80** in the **Distance** box.

20. Click **OK** to explode the Key.

Creating Tracelines

1. To create tracelines, click **Exploded Views > Tracelines** on the ribbon.

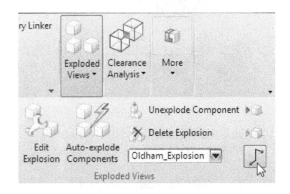

21. Activate the **Edit Explosion** dialog.

22. Explode the shaft in Y-direction upto to a distance of **-80 mm**.

2. Click on the center point of the Flange.

3. On the **Tracelines** dialog, select **End Object > Point**.

4. Click on the center point of the circular edge of the shaft.

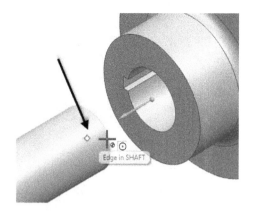

5. Click **OK** to create the trace line.

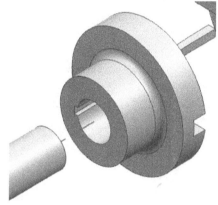

6. Click the **Tracelines** button on the **Exploded Views** group.

7. Under the **Start** section, select **Inferred > End Point**.

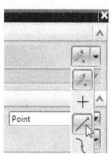

8. Select the edge on the key way of the shaft.

9. Double-click on the arrow displayed on the edge to reverse the direction.

10. Under the **End** section, select **Inferred > End Point**.

11. Click on the edge on the key.

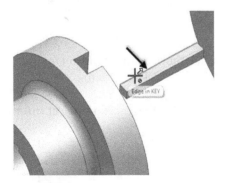

12. Double-click on the arrow to reverse the direction.

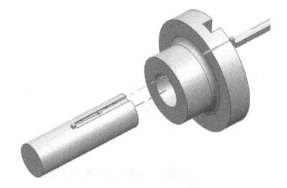

13. Click **OK** to create the traceline.

14. Create tracelines between the other parts.

15. Change the view to **Wireframe with Hidden Edges**.

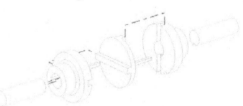

16. Click **Save** on the **Quick Access Toolbar,** or click **File > Save**.

17. Close the file.

Chapter 4: Generating Drawings

In this chapter, you generate drawings of the parts and assembly from previous chapters.

You will:

- Open and edit a drawing template
- Insert standard views of a part model
- Add model and reference annotations
- Create a custom template
- Insert exploded view of the assembly
- Insert a bill of materials of the assembly
- Apply balloons to the assembly

TUTORIAL 1

In this tutorial, you will generate drawings of Flange constructed in previous chapters.

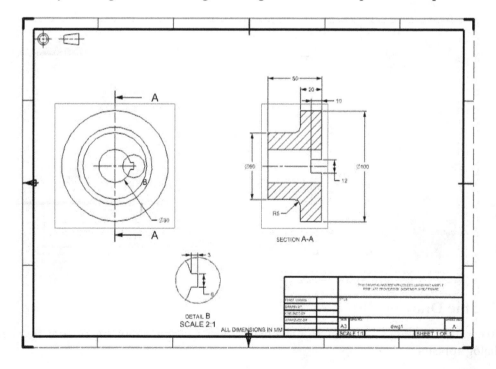

NX 9 Tutorial

Opening a New Drawing File

1. Start NX 9.

2. To open a new drawing, click the **New** button on the **Standard** group, or click **File > New**.

3. On the **New** dialog, select the **Drawing** tab.

4. Click **A3-Size** in the **Templates** section.

5. Click **OK**.

6. On the **Populate Title Block** dialog, select the individual labels and type-in their values.

7. Click the **Close** button.

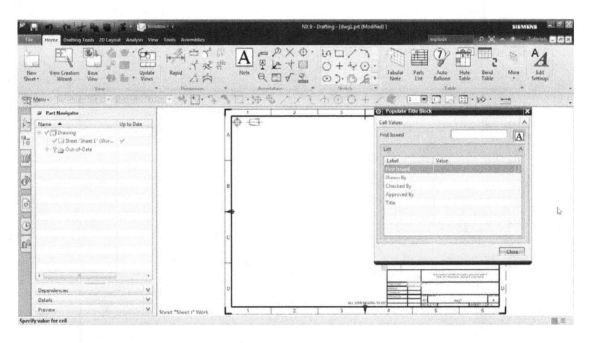

Editing the Drawing Sheet

1. To edit the drawing sheet, click **Home > New Sheet > Edit Sheet** on the ribbon; the **Sheet** dialog appears.

2. Click the **More** button (three down-arrows) displayed at the bottom of the dialog. The **Settings** section appears.

3. Set **Units** to **Millimeters**.

4. Set the **Projection** type to **3rd Angle Projection**.

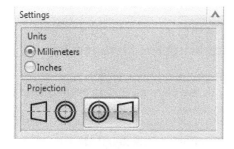

5. Click **OK** on the **Sheet** dialog.

Generating the Base View

1. To generate the base view, click **Base View** on the **View** group.

2. On the **Base View** message box, click

Yes.

3. On the **Part Name** dialog, browse to the location NX 9/C3/Oldham_Coupling, and then double-click on **Flange.prt**. The **Base View** dialog appears.

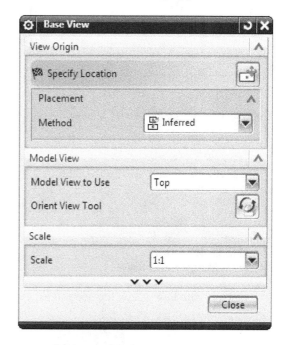

In addition, the view appears along with the cursor.

4. Under the **Model View** section, select **Model View to Use > Front**.

5. Place the view, as shown in figure.

6. On the **Projected View** dialog, click **Close**.

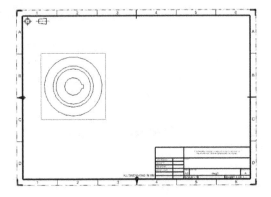

Generating the Section View

1. To generate the section view, click
   Home > View > Section View Drop-
   down **> Section View** on the ribbon.

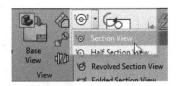

2. Click on the base view; the section line
   appears.

3. Click on the center point of the base
   view.

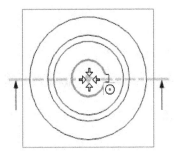

4. Drag the cursor toward right and click
   to position the section view.

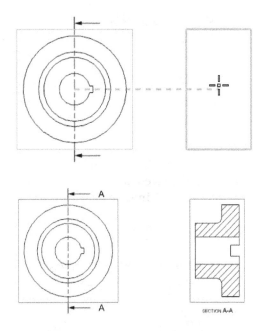

Generating the Detailed View

Now, you need to generate the detailed
view of the keyway that appears on the
front view.

1. To generate the detailed view, click
   Detail View button on the **View** group.

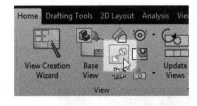

2. On the **Detail View** dialog, select **Type
   > Circular**.

3. Specify the center point and boundary
   point of the detail view, as shown in
   figure.

NX 9 Tutorial

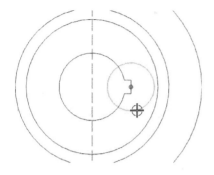

4. Under the **Scale** section, select **Scale >
   2:1**.

5. Position the detail view below the base
   view.

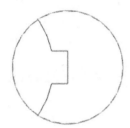

DETAIL **B**
SCALE 2:1

6. Click **Close**.

Adding Center Marks and Centerlines

1. To add a center mark on the front view,
   click **Home > Annotation > Center
   Mark** on the ribbon.

2. Click on the hole at the center of the

front view.

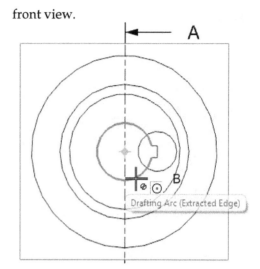

3. Click **OK** to add the center mark.

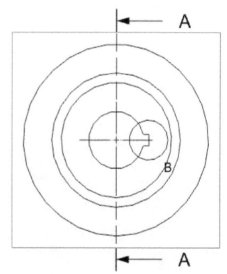

4. To add a centerline to the section view,
   click **Home > Annotation > Centerline
   Drop-down > 3D Centerline** on the
   ribbon.

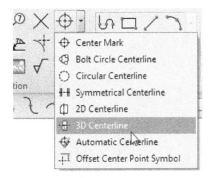

5. Click on the horizontal edges of the section view, as shown in figure.

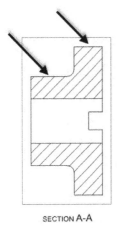

SECTION A-A

6. Click **OK** to add the centerline.

SECTION A-A

Setting the Annotation Preferences

1. To set the annotation preferences, click **File > Preferences > Drafting**.

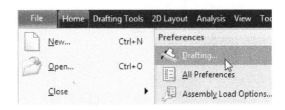

2. On the **Drafting Preferences** dialog, click **Dimension > Text > Orientation and Location**.

3. Set the **Orientation** value to **Horizontal Text**.

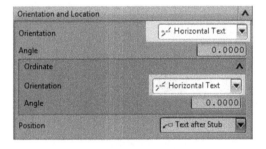

4. On the dialog, click **Dimension > Text > Units**.

5. Set the **Decimal Delimiter** value to **. Period**.

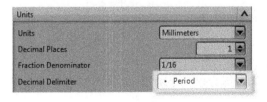

6. On the dialog, click **Dimension > Text > Dimension Text**.

7. Under the **Format** section, type-in **3.5** in the **Height** box.

8. Click **Common > Line/Arrow > Arrowhead**.

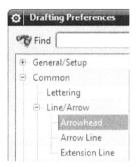

9. Under the **Workflow** section, uncheck the **Automatic Orientation** option.

10. Under the **Format** section, type-in **3.5** and **30** in the **Length** and **Angle** boxes, respectively.

11. Click **Common > Line/Arrow > Extension Line**.

12. Type-in **1** in the **Gap** boxes.

13. Type in **2** in the **Extension Line Overhang**.

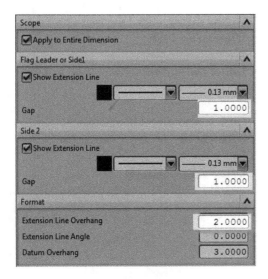

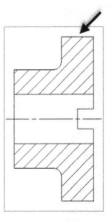

SECTION A-A

14. Click **Common > Line/Arrow > Lettering**.

15. Under the **Text Parameters** section, type-in **3.5** in **Height** box,

16. Click **OK**.

3. Drag the cursor up and click to position the dimension.

Dimensioning the Drawing Views

1. To add dimensions, click **Home > Dimension > Rapid Dimension** on the ribbon.

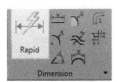

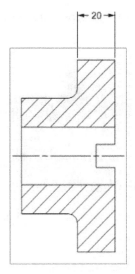

SECTION A-A

4. Click on the ends of the section view, as shown.

2. On the section view, click the horizontal line located at the top.

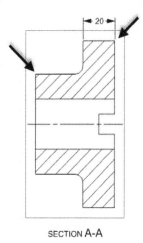

SECTION A-A

5. Drag the cursor up and click to position the dimension.

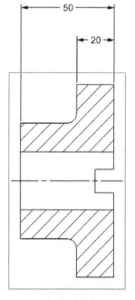

SECTION A-A

6. Add another linear dimension on the section view.

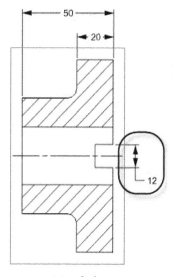

SECTION A-A

7. On the section view, click on the arc locate at the bottom.

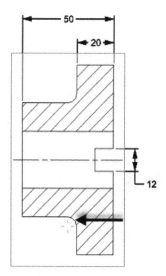

SECTION A-A

8. Drag the cursor downward and click to position the radial dimension.

61

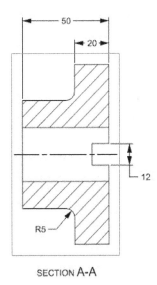

SECTION A-A

11. Drag the mouse rightwards and click to position the dimension.

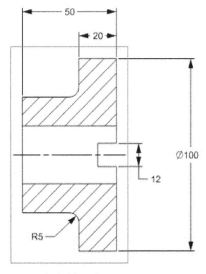

SECTION A-A

9. On the **Rapid Dimension** dialog, under the **Measurement** section, select **Method > Cylindrical**.

12. Create the other dimensions on the section view, as shown.

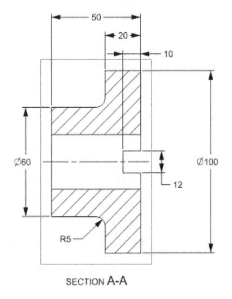

SECTION A-A

10. Click on the ends of the section view, as shown.

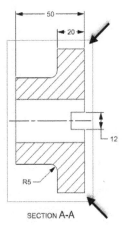

SECTION A-A

NX 9 Tutorial

13. Create the hole dimension on the front view, as shown.

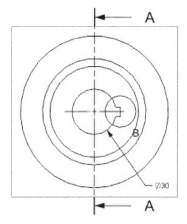

14. Create the dimensions on the detail view, as shown.

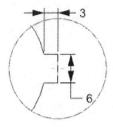

DETAIL B
SCALE 2:1

Saving the Drawing

1. On the **Quick Access Toolbar**, click **Save**.

2. On the **Name Parts** dialog, type-in **Flange Drawing** in the **Name** box and click **Folder** button.

3. Browse to NX 9/C4 folder, and then click **OK** button twice

4. Close the drawing.

TUTORIAL 2

In this tutorial, you generate the drawing of the Disc constructed in Chapter 1.

Creating a custom template

1. Close the NX 9 application window.

2. Click **Start > All Programs > Siemens NX 9.0**.

3. Click the right mouse button on NX 9.0 and select **Run as administrator**.

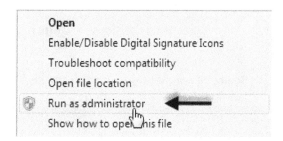

4. On the ribbon, click the **New** button.

5. On the **New** dialog, double-click on the **Model** template.

6. Click **File > Applications > Drafting**.

NX 9 Tutorial

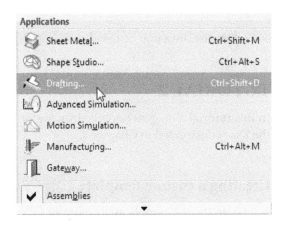

7. On the **Sheet** dialog, select **Standard Size**.

8. Set **Size** to **A3 – 297 x 420**.

9. Set **Scale** to **1:1**.

10. Under the **Settings** section, set **Units** to **Millimeters**.

11. Select **3rd Angle Projection** and uncheck **Always Start View Creation**.

12. Click **OK** to open a blank sheet.

Adding Borders and Title Block

1. On the ribbon, click **Drafting Tools > Drawing Format > Borders and Zones** on the ribbon.

2. On the **Borders and Zones** dialog, leave

the default settings and click **OK**.

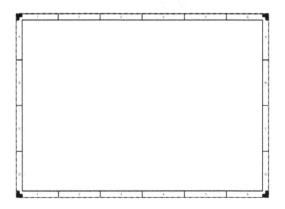

3. On the ribbon, click **Home > Table > Tabular Note**.

4. On the **Tabular Note** dialog, under the **Origin** section, expand the **Alignment** section and select **Anchor > Bottom Right**.

5. Under the **Table Size** section, set **Number of Columns** to **3** and **Number of Rows** to **2**.

6. Type-in **50** in **Column Width** box.

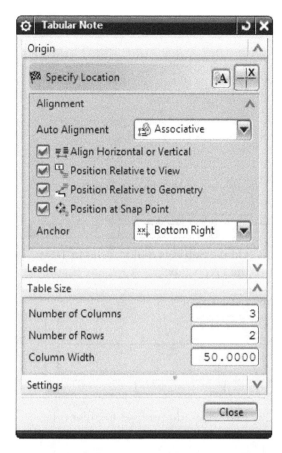

10. Press the left mouse button and drag toward right.

11. Release the left mouse button when column width is changed to 35.

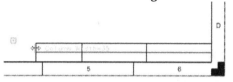

12. Likewise, change the width of the second and third columns.

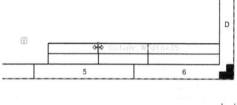

13. Change the height of the top row.

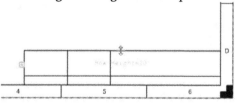

7. Click on the bottom right corner of the sheet border.

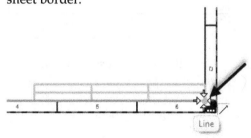

8. Click **Close** on the **Tabular Note** dialog.

9. Click on the left vertical line of the tabular note.

14. Click inside the second cell of the top row.

15. Press the left mouse button and drag to

the third cell.

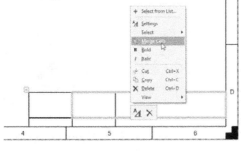

16. Click the right mouse button and select **Merge Cells**.

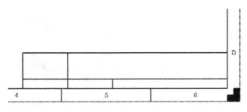

17. Click the right mouse button in the second cell of the top row. Select **Settings**.

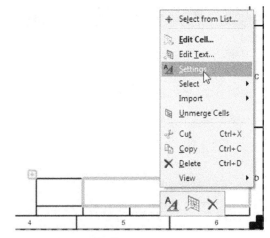

18. On the **Settings** dialog, type-in **Title:** in the **Prefix** box.

19. Click **Close**.

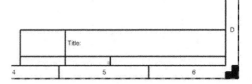

20. Likewise, add prefixes to other cells.

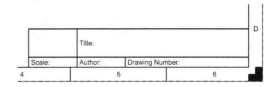

21. Click the right mouse button in the first cell of the top row.

22. Click **Import > Image**.

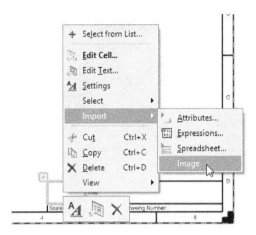

23. Select your company logo image and click **OK.**

24. On the ribbon, click **Drafting Tools > Drawing Format > Define Title Block**.

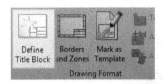

25. Click on the table, and then click **OK**.

26. On the ribbon, click **Drafting Tools > Drawing Format > Mark as Template**.

27. On the dialog, select **Mark as Template and Update PAX File**.

28. Under the **PAX File Settings** section, type-in **Custom Template** in the **Presentation Name** box.

29. Select **Template Type > Reference Existing Part**.

30. Click the **Browse** icon.

31. Go to *C:\Program Files\Siemens\NX 9.0\LOCALIZATION\prc\english\startup*

32. Click **ugs_drawing_templates**.

33. Click **OK**.

34. On the **Input Validation** box, click **Yes**.

35. Click **OK**.

36. On the ribbon, click **Home > Track Drawing Changes > Create Snapshot Data**.

37. Save and close the file.

Opening a new drawing file using the custom template

1. On the ribbon, click the **New** button.

2. On the **New** dialog, under the **Drawing** tab, select **Relationship > Reference Existing Part**.

3. Under the **Templates** section, select **Custom Template**.

4. Under the **Part to create a drawing of** section, click the **Browse** button.

5. On the **Select master part** dialog, click **Open**.

6. Go to the location of Disc.prt and double-click on it.

7. Click **OK** twice.

8. On the **Populate Title Block** dialog, type-in values, as shown.

9. Click **Close**.

Generating Drawing Views

1. On the **View Creation Wizard** dialog, select **Loaded Parts > Disc.prt**.

2. Click **Next**.

3. On the **Options** page, select **View Boundary > Manual**.

4. Uncheck the **Auto-Scale to Fit** option.

5. Select **Scale > 1:1**.

6. Select **Hidden Lines > Dashed**.

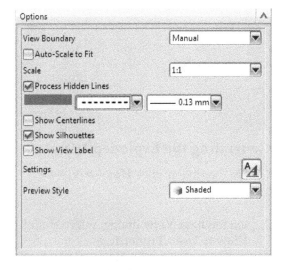

7. Click **Next**.

8. On the **Orientation** page, select **Model Views > Front**.

9. Click **Next**.

10. On the **Layout** page, select the view, as shown.

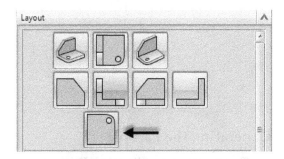

11. Select **Option > Manual**.

12. Click to define the center of the views, as shown.

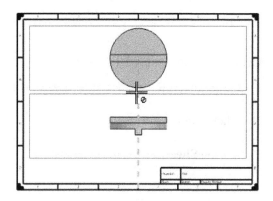

Adding Dimensions

1. Add centerlines and dimensions to the drawing.

2. Save and close the drawing file.

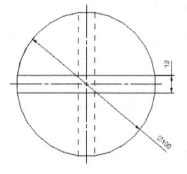

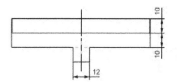

TUTORIAL 3

In this tutorial, you generate the drawing of Oldham coupling assembly created in the previous chapter.

Creating the assembly drawing

1. Open the Main_assembly.prt file.

2. Click **File > Applications > Drafting**.

3. On the **Sheet** dialog, select **Standard Size**.

4. Set **Size** to **A3 -297 x 420**.

5. Set **Scale** to **1:2**.

6. Under the **Settings** section, select **Base View command**.

7. Click **OK**.

8. On the **Base View** dialog, under the **Model View** section, select **Model View to Use > Isometric**.

9. Under the **Scale** section, select **Scale > 1:2**.

10. Click on the left side of the drawing sheet.

11. Click **Close** on the **Projected View** dialog.

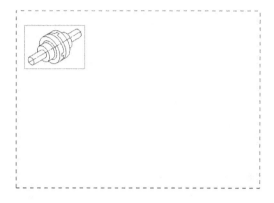

Generating the Exploded View

1. On the ribbon, click **Home > View > Base View**.

2. On the **Base View** dialog, select **Model View to Use >Trimetric**.

3. Click on the right side of the drawing sheet.

4. Click **Close**.

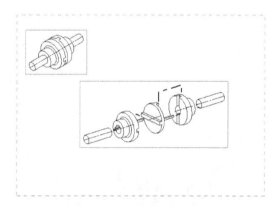

Generating the Part list

1. To generate a part list, click **Home > Table > Part List** on the ribbon.

70

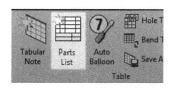

2. Place the part list at the top-right corner.

Generating Balloons

1. To generate balloons, click **Home >
   Table > Auto Balloon** on ribbon.

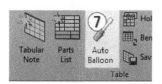

2. Select the part list.

3. Click **OK**.

4. On the **Part List Auto-Balloon** dialog,
   select **Trimetric@2**.

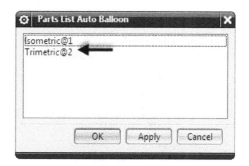

5. Click **OK** to generate balloons.

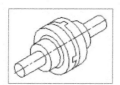

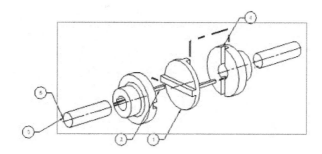

6. Save and close the file.

Chapter 5: Additional Modeling Tools

In this chapter, you will:

- Construct a Sweep feature
- Construct a Swept feature along guide curves
- Create Holes
- Add Grooves and Slots
- Make Pattern Features
- Construct Tube features
- Construct Instance Geometry
- Apply Boolean operations
- Construct Ribs
- Add chamfers

TUTORIAL 1

In this tutorial, you will construct a helical spring using the **Helix** and **Sweep along Guide** tools.

Constructing the Helix

1. Open a NX file using the **Model** template.

2. To construct a helix, click **Curve > Curve > Helix** on the ribbon.

3. On the **Helix** dialog, select **Type >
   Along Vector**.

4. Select the coordinate system from the
   graphics window.

5. Specify the settings in the **Size** section,
   as given next.

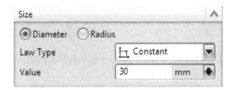

6. Specify the settings in the **Pitch** section,
   as given next.

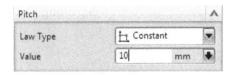

7. Specify the settings in the **Length**
   section, as given next.

8. Expand the dialog and specify the
   settings in the **Settings** section, as given
   next.

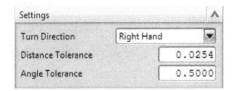

9. Click **OK** to construct the helix.

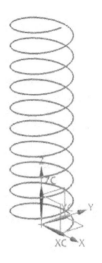

Adding the Datum Plane

1. To add a datum plane, click **Home >
   Feature > Datum Plane** on the ribbon.

2. On the **Datum Plane** dialog, select **Type
   > On Curve**.

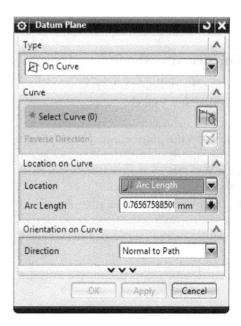

3. Select the helix from the graphics window.

4. Under the **Location on Curve** section, select **Location > Through Point**.

5. Select the end of the helix.

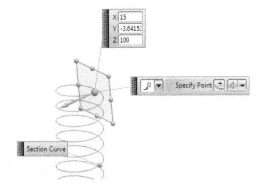

6. Under the **Orientation on Curve** section, select **Direction > Normal to Path**.

7. Leave the default values and click **OK**.

Constructing the Sweep feature

1. On the ribbon, click **Home > Direct Sketch > Sketch**.

2. Select the plane created normal to helix.

3. Click **OK**.

4. Draw circle of 4 mm diameter.

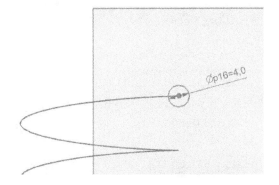

5. Right-click and select **Finish Sketch.**

6. On Top Border Bar, click the **Orient View > Isometric**.

7. To construct a sweep feature, click **Surface > More > Sweep along Guide** on the ribbon.

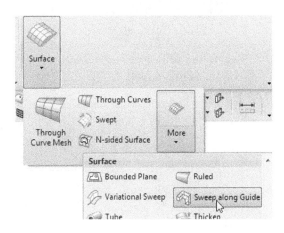

8. Select the circle to define the section curve.

9. Under the **Guide** section, click **Select Curve**.

10. Select the helix.

11. Leave the default settings and click **OK** to construct the sweep feature.

12. Click on the plane and select **Hide**.

Also, hide the sketches.

1. Open a file in the **Modeling** Environment.

2. Construct the sketch on the YZ plane, as shown in figure.

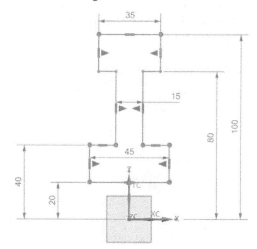

13. Save and close the file.

TUTORIAL 2

In this tutorial, you construct a pulley wheel using the **Revolve** and **Groove** tools.

3. Construct the revolved feature.

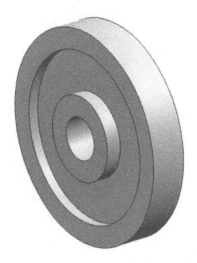

Constructing the Groove feature

1. To construct a groove feature, click
   **Home > Feature > Design Feature >
   Groove** on the ribbon.

Note
Some tools do not appear on the ribbon. To
display the required tools, select them from
the menu, as shown in figure.

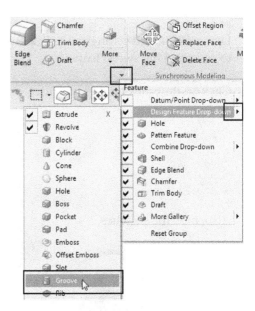

2. On the **Groove** dialog, click the **U
   Groove** button.

3. Select the outer cylindrical face of the
   revolved feature.

4. Specify the values on the **U Groove**
   dialog, as shown in figure.

5. Click **OK**; the **Position Groove** dialog appears.

6. Click on the cylindrical edges of the model and groove preview, as shown.

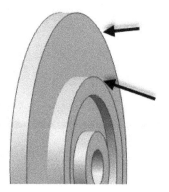

7. Enter **7.5** on the **Create Expression** dialog.

8. Click **OK** to add the groove.

9. Click **Cancel**.

10. Save and close the model.

TUTORIAL 3

In this tutorial, you construct a shampoo bottle using the **Swept**, **Extrude**, and **Thread** tools.

NX 9 Tutorial

Creating Sections and Guide curves

To construct a swept feature, you need to create sections and guide curves.

1. Open a new file in the **Modeling** Environment.

2. On the ribbon, click **Home > Direct Sketch > Sketch**.

3. Select the XY plane.

4. On the **Create Sketch** dialog, click **OK** to start the sketch.

5. On the ribbon, click **Home > Direct Sketch > Ellipse**.

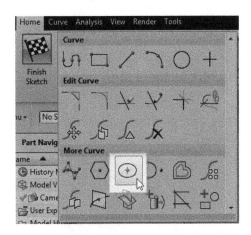

6. Select the origin point of the sketch.

7. Specify **Major Radius** as 50 mm.

8. Specify **Minor Radius** as 20 mm.

9. Specify **Angle** as 0.

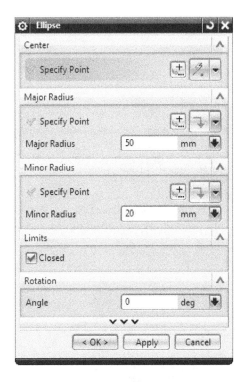

10. Leave the default settings and click **OK**.

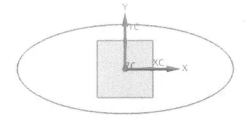

11. Click **Finish Sketch**.

12. Change the orientation to Isometric.

13. On the ribbon, click **Home > Direct Sketch > Sketch**.

14. Select the XZ plane.

15. Click **OK**.

16. On the ribbon, click **Home > Direct Sketch > Studio Spline**.

17. On the **Studio Spline** dialog, select **Type > Through Points**.

18. Draw a spline similarly to the one shown in figure.

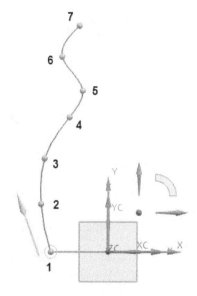

Ensure that the first point of the spline coincides with the previous sketch.

16. Click **OK**.

17. Apply dimension to the spline, as shown in figure.

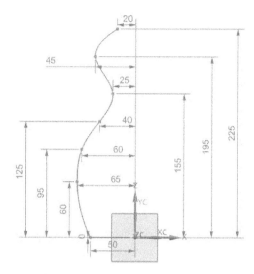

18. On the ribbon, click **Home > Direct Sketch > Mirror Curve**.

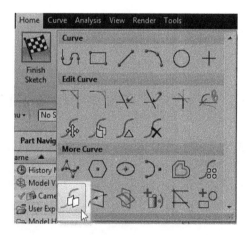

19. Select the spline.

20. On the **Mirror Curve** dialog, click **Select Centerline**, and then select the vertical axis of the sketch.

21. Click **OK**.

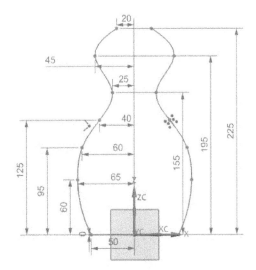

22. Click **Finish Sketch**.

23. Change the view orientation to Isometric.

Creating another section

1. On the ribbon, click **Home > Feature > Datum Plane**.

2. On the **Datum Plane** dialog, select **Type > At Distance**.

3. Select the XY plane from the coordinate system.

4. Type-in **225** in the **Distance** box.

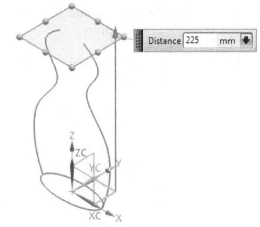

5. Click **OK**.

6. Start a sketch on the new datum plane.

7. Draw a circle of 40 mm diameter.

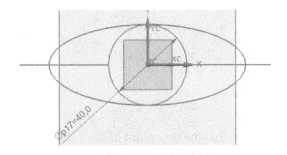

8. Click **Finish Sketch**.

9. Change the view to Isometric.

Constructing the swept feature.

1. On the ribbon, click **Home > Surface > Swept**.

NX 9 Tutorial

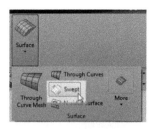

2. Select the circle and click the middle mouse button.

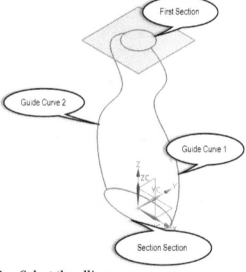

3. Select the ellipse.

Ensure that the arrows on the circle and the ellipse point are in the same direction. Use the **Reverse Direction** button in the **Sections** section to reverse the direction of arrows.

8. Click **Select Curve** in the **Guides (3 maximum)** section.

9. Select the first guide curve and click the middle mouse button.

10. Select the second guide curve.

11. Click **OK** to construct the swept feature.

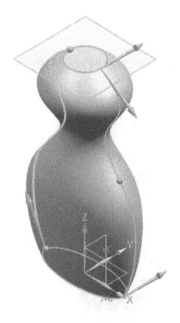

Constructing the Extruded feature

1. Click on the circle on the top of the sweep feature.

2. Click **Extrude** on the contextual toolbar.

3. On the **Extrude** dialog, under the **Boolean** section, select **Boolean > Unite**.

NX 9 Tutorial

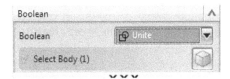

4. Extrude the circle upto 25 mm.

Adding the Emboss feature

1. On the **Feature** group, click the **Datum Plane** button.

2. On the **Datum Plane** dialog, select **Type > At Distance**.

3. Select the XZ plane from the coordinate system.

4. Type-in **50** in the **Distance** box.

5. Click **Reverse Direction** to create the plane, as shown. Click **OK**.

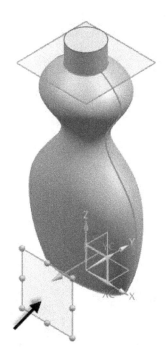

6. Create a sketch on the plane, as shown in figure. The major and minor radii of the ellipse are 50 and 20, respectively.

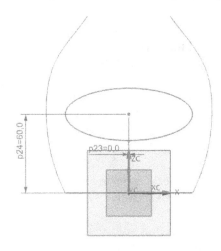

6. Click **Finish Sketch**.

7. On the ribbon, add the **Emboss** tool to the **Feature** group.

8. On the ribbon, click **Home > Feature > Design Feature > Emboss**.

9. Select the sketch.

10. On the **Emboss** dialog, under **Face to Emboss**, click **Select Face**.

11. Select the swept feature.

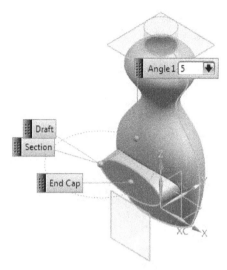

12. Under the **End Cap** section, specify the settings in, as given in figure.

13. Leave the default settings and click **OK** to add the embossed feature.

NX 9 Tutorial

Adding Edge Blends

1. On the ribbon, click **Home > Feature > Edge Blend**.

2. Click on the bottom and top edges of the swept feature.

3. Set **Radius 1** to 5 mm.

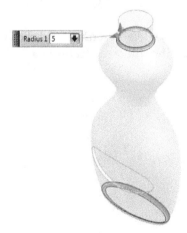

4. Click **Apply** to add the blend.

5. Set **Radius 1** to 1 mm.

6. Select the edges of the emboss feature and click **OK**.

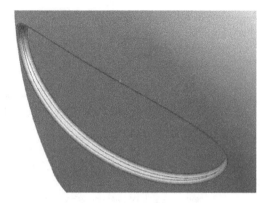

Shelling the Model

1. On the ribbon, click **Home > Feature > Shell**.

2. On the **Shell** dialog, select **Type > Remove Faces, then Shell**.

3. Set **Thickness** to 2 mm.

4. Select the top face of the cylindrical feature.

84

5. Click **OK** to shell the geometry.

4. Set **Pitch** to 8 mm.

Adding Threads

1. On the ribbon, click **Home > Feature > More > Thread**.

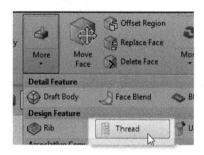

5. Leave the other default settings and click **OK** to add the thread.

2. On the **Thread** dialog, set **Thread Type** to **Detailed**.

3. Select the cylindrical face.

6. Save the model and close it.

TUTORIAL 4

In this tutorial, you construct a patterned cylindrical shell.

Constructing a cylindrical shell

1. Start a new file using the **Model** template.

2. On the Top Border Bar, click **Menu > Insert > Design Feature > Cylinder**.

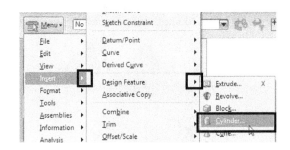

3. On the **Cylinder** dialog, select **Type > Axis, Diameter, and Height**.

4. Select the Z-axis from the triad.

5. Set **Diameter** and **Height** to **50** and **100**, respectively.

6. Leave the default settings and click **OK**.

7. On the ribbon, click **Home > Feature > Shell**.

8. Set **Thickness** to 3 mm.

9. Select the top and bottom faces of the cylindrical feature.

10. Click **OK** to shell the geometry.

Adding slots

1. On Top Border Bar, click **Menu > Insert > Design Feature > Slot**.

2. On the **Slot** dialog, select **Rectangle,** and then click **OK**.

3. Click on the YZ plane.

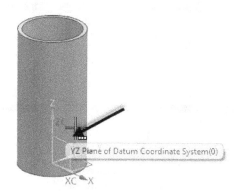

4. Click **Flip Default Side**.

5. Select Z-axis from the Datum Coordinate System.

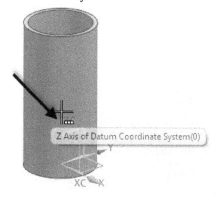

6. On the **Rectangular Slot** dialog, type-in 8, 3, and 30 in the **Length**, **Width** and **Depth** boxes, respectively.

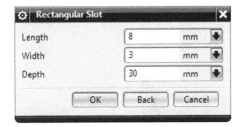

7. Click **OK**.

   The **Positioning** dialog appears. In addition, the slot tool appears.

8. On the **Positioning** dialog, click the **Horizontal** button.

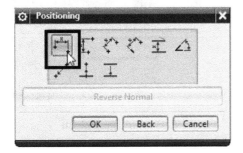

9. Select the circular edge of the cylindrical feature.

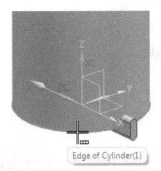

10. On the **Set Arc Position** dialog, click **Arc Center** on the dialog.

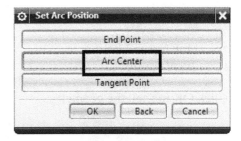

11. Select the circular edge on the slot tool.

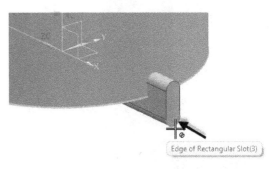

12. On the **Set Arc Position** dialog, click **Arc Center**.

13. Enter -8 mm in the dialog.

14. Click **OK** twice to add the slot feature.

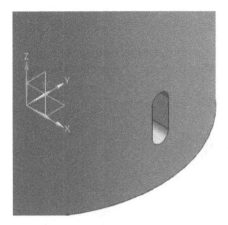

15. Click **Cancel**.

Constructing the Linear pattern

1. On the ribbon, click **Home > Feature > Pattern Feature**.

2. On the **Pattern Feature** dialog, select **Layout > Linear**.

3. Select the slot feature.

4. Under the **Pattern Definition** section, select **Direction 1 > Specify Vector**.

5. Select the Z-axis vector.

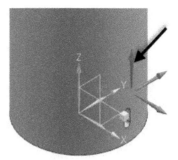

6. Select **Spacing > Count and Pitch**.

7. Type-in **6** in the **Count** box.

8. Enter **16** in the **Pitch Distance** box.

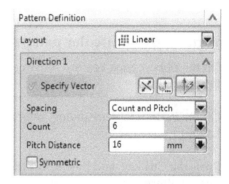

9. Click **OK** to make the linear pattern.

NX 9 Tutorial

Constructing the Circular pattern

1. On the ribbon, click **Feature > Pattern Feature**

2. On the **Pattern Feature** dialog, select **Layout > Circular**.

3. Press the Ctrl key, and then select the linear pattern and the slot feature from the **Part Navigator**.

4. Under the **Pattern Definition** section, select **Rotation Axis > Specify Vector**.

5. Select the Z-axis vector.

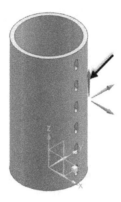

Now, you have to specify the point through which the rotation axis passes.

6. Click on the circular edge of the cylindrical feature (to select the center point of the cylinder).

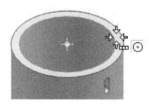

7. Select **Spacing > Count and Span**.

8. Type-in **12** in the **Count** box.

9. Type-in **360** in the **Span Angle** box.

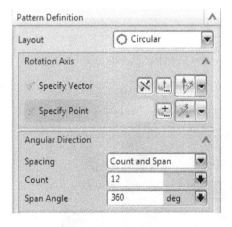

10. Click **OK** to make the circular pattern.

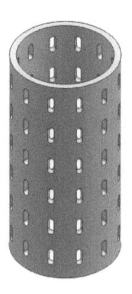

11. Save and close the model.

TUTORIAL 5

In this tutorial, you will construct a chain.

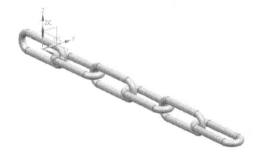

Constructing the Tube feature

1. Open a new file using the **Model** template.

2. On the ribbon, click **Home > Direct Sketch > Sketch**.

3. Select the XZ plane.

NX 9 Tutorial

4. Click OK.

5. On the ribbon, click **Home > Direct Sketch > Profile**.

6. Click on the screen to define the first point.

7. Drag the cursor rightwards and click to define the second point.

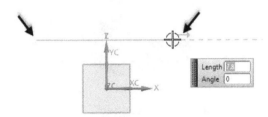

8. On the **Profile** dialog, click **Arc**.

9. Drag the mouse toward right, and then downwards.

10. Click to draw the arc.

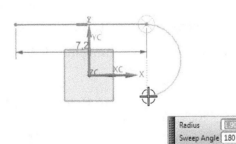

11. Drag the mouse toward left and click to define a horizontal line.

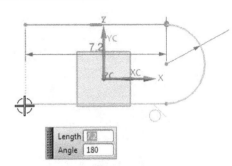

12. On the **Profile** dialog, click **Arc**.

13. Drag the mouse toward left, and then upwards.

14. Click on the start point of the sketch to draw the arc

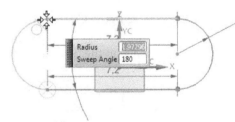

15. Close the **Profile** dialog.

16. On the ribbon, click **Home > Direct Sketch > More > Make Symmetric**.

17. Select the two arcs and click on the vertical axis.

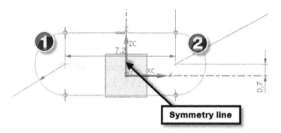

Symmetry line

18. Click **Reset** on the **Make Symmetric** dialog.

19. Select the horizontal lines, and then click on the horizontal axis.

20. Click **Close**.

21. Add dimensions to the sketch.

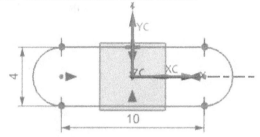

22. Click **Finish Sketch** on the **Direct Sketch** group.

23. To construct a tube feature, click **Home > Surface > More > Tube** on the ribbon.

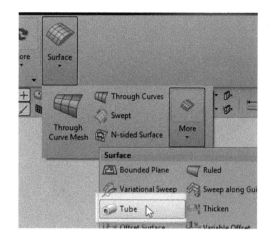

24. Select the sketch.

25. On the **Tube** dialog, type-in 1.5 and 0 in the **Outer Diameter** and **Inner Diameter** boxes, respectively.

26. Click **OK** to construct the tube feature.

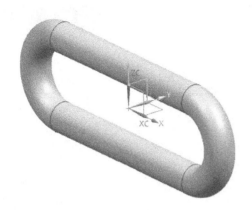

Patterning the Tube geometry

1. On the ribbon, click **Home > Feature > Pattern Feature**.

2. On the **Pattern Feature** dialog, select **Layout > Linear** and click on the tube feature.

3. Under the **Pattern Definition** section, select **Direction 1 > Specify Vector**.

4. Select the X-axis vector.

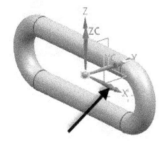

5. Under **Direction 1**, select **Spacing > Count and Pitch**.

6. Type-in **6** and **12** in the **Count** and **Pitch** boxes, respectively.

7. Expand the **Orientation** section and select **Orientation > CSYS to CSYS**.

8. Under **Orientation**, select **Specify From Vector CSYS > CSYS Dialog**.

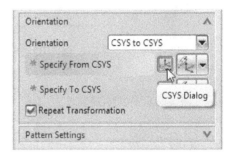

9. On the **CSYS** dialog, select **Type > Dynamic**.

10. Accept the default position of the Dynamic CSYS and click **OK**.

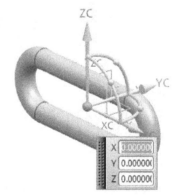

11. On the **Pattern Feature** dialog, under **Orientation**, select **Specify To CSYS > CSYS Dialog**.

12. Rotate the Dynamic CSYS about the X-axis. The rotation angle is -90 degrees.

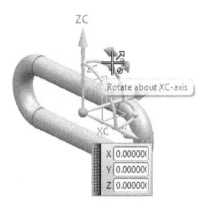

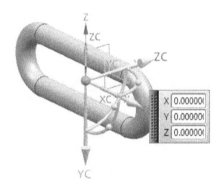

13. Click **OK**.

14. On the **Pattern Feature** dialog, under **Orientation**, check the **Repeat Transformation** option.

15. Click **OK** to make pattern of the tube.

16. On the Top Border Bar, click **Fit**.

17. Save and close the file.

Boolean Operations

Types of boolean operations.

Unite
Subtract
Intersect

These tools combine, subtract, or intersect two bodies. Activate these tools from the **Combine** drop-down on the **Feature** group.

Unite: This tool combines the **Tool Body** and the **Target Body** into a single body.

Subtract: This tool subtracts the **Tool body** from the **Target body**.

Intersect: This tool keeps the intersecting portion of the tool and target bodies.

TUTORIAL 6

In this tutorial, you will construct the model shown in figure.

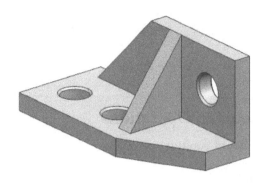

Constructing the first feature

1. Open a new part file.

2. Construct the first feature on the XY plane (extrude the sketch upto a distance of 10 mm).

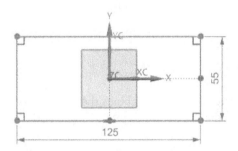

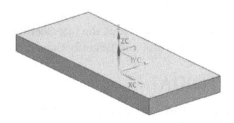

Constructing the Second Feature

1. Draw the sketch on the top face of the first feature.

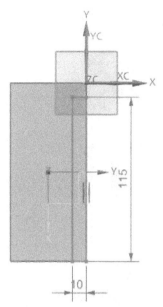

2. On the ribbon, click **Home > Feature > Extrude**.

3. Select the sketch.

4. Type-in **45** in the **End** box.

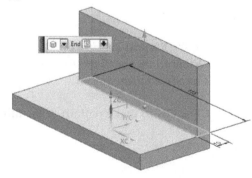

5. Under the **Boolean** section, select **Boolean > Unite**.

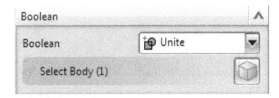

6. Click **OK**.

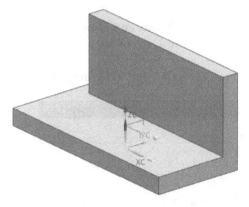

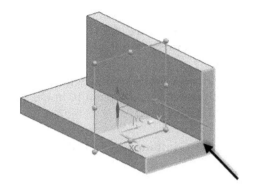

5. Click **OK**.

6. Draw the sketch on the new datum plane.

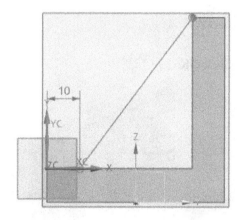

Constructing the third feature

1. On the ribbon, click **Home > Feature > Datum Plane**.

2. On the **Datum Plane** dialog, select **Type > At Distance**.

3. Click on the right-side face of the model geometry.

4. Type-in **50** in the **Distance** box and click the **Reverse Direction** icon on the **Datum Plane** dialog.

7. On the ribbon, click **Home > Feature > More > Rib**.

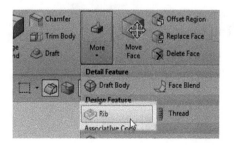

8. Select the sketch.

9. On the **Rib** dialog, select **Walls > Parallel to Section Plane**.

10. Under the **Walls** section, select **Distance > Symmetric** and type-in **10** in the **Thickness** box.

11. Check **Combine Rib with Target**.

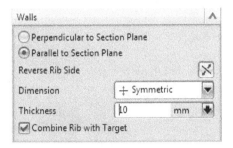

12. Click **OK**.

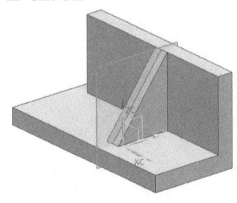

Drilling Holes

1. To drill holes, click **Home > Feature > Hole** on the ribbon.

2. On the **Hole** dialog, select **Type > Drill Size Hole**.

3. Under the **Forms and Dimensions** section, select **Size > 16**.

4. Select **Depth Limit > Through Body**.

5. Click on the top face of the model.

NX 9 Tutorial

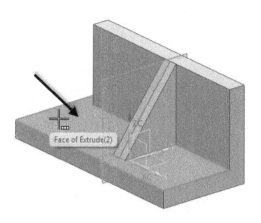

6. Click to place one more point.

7. Click **Close** on the **Sketch Point** dialog.

8. Add dimensions to define the hole location.

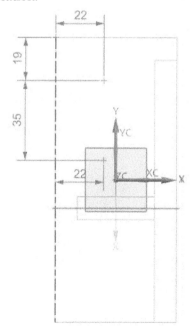

9. Click **Finish** on the ribbon.

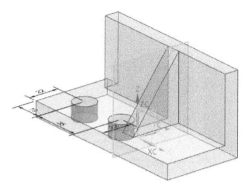

10. Click **Apply** to create the hole.

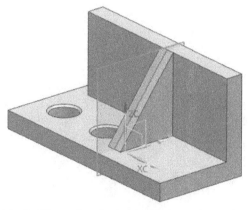

11. Drill another hole on the front face of the second feature.

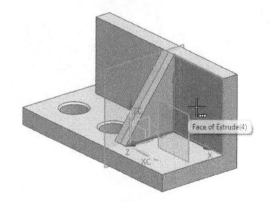

NX 9 Tutorial

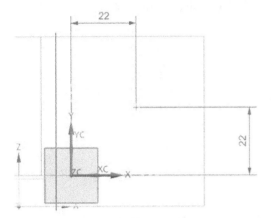

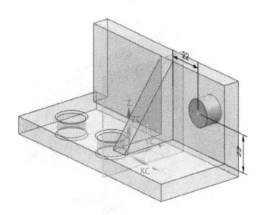

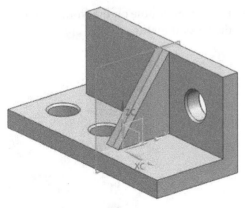

Adding Chamfers

1. To add a chamfer, click **Home > Feature > Chamfer** on the ribbon.

2. On the **Chamfer** dialog, select **Cross Section > Asymmetric**.

3. Under the **Offsets** section, type-in **25** and **45** in the **Distance 1** and **Distance 2** boxes.

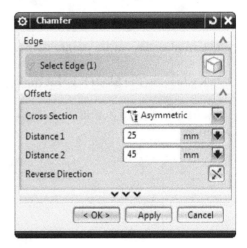

4. Click on the corner edge of the first feature.

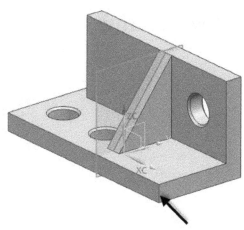

5. Click **Apply** add the chamfer.

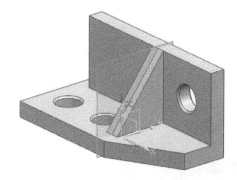

6. On the **Chamfer** dialog, select **Cross Section > Symmetric**.

7. Type-in **45** in the **Distance** box.

8. Click on the corner edge of the second feature.

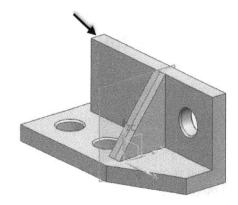

9. Click **OK**.

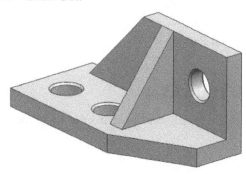

10. Save the model.

11. Close the file.

Chapter 6: Sheet metal Modeling

This chapter will show you to:

- Construct Tab feature
- Construct Flange
- Contour Flange
- Closed corners
- Louvers
- Beads
- Drawn Cutouts
- Gussets
- Flat Pattern

TUTORIAL 1

In this tutorial, you construct the sheet metal model shown in figure.

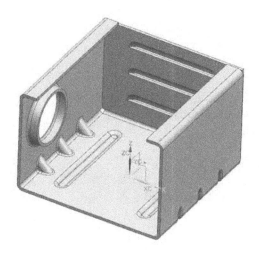

Opening a New Sheet metal File

1. To open a new sheet metal file, click **Home > New** on the ribbon.

2. On the **New** dialog, click **Sheet Metal**.

3. Click **OK**.

The Sheet Metal ribbon appears, as shown below.

Setting the Parameters of the Sheet Metal part

1. To set the parameters, click **File > Preferences > Sheet Metal**

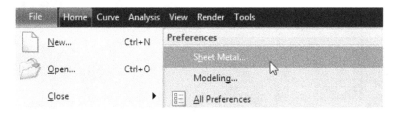

On the **NX Sheet Metal Preferences** dialog, , you can set the preferences of the sheet metal part such as thickness, bend radius, relief depth, width and so on. In this tutorial, you will construct the sheet metal part with the default preferences.

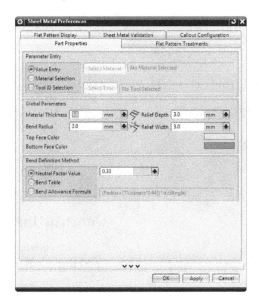

Constructing the Tab Feature

1. To construct the tab feature, click **Home > Basic > Tab** on the ribbon.

2. Select the XY plane.

3. Construct the sketch, as shown.

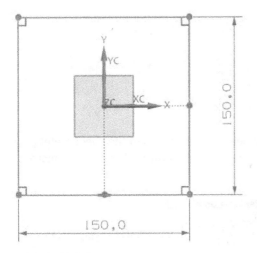

4. Click **Finish**.

5. Click **OK** to construct the tab feature.

Adding a flange

1. To add the flange, click **Home > Bend > Flange** on the ribbon.

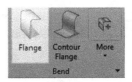

2. Select the edge on the top face.

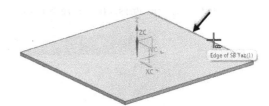

3. Set **Length** to 100.

4. Click **OK** to add the flange.

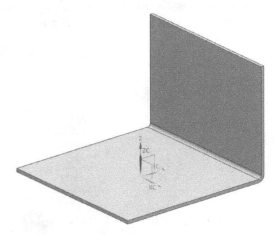

Constructing the Contour Flange

1. To construct the contour flange, click **Home > Bend > Contour Flange** on the ribbon.

2. On the **Contour Flange** dialog, click the **Sketch Section** icon.

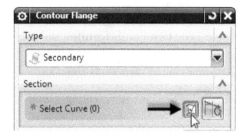

3. On the Top Border Bar, select **Curve Rule > Single Curve**.

4. Click the edge on the left side of the top face.

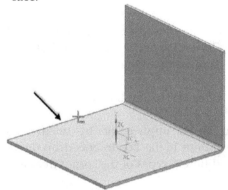

5. On the **Create Sketch** dialog, under the **Plane Location** section, type-in **100** in the **% Arc Length** box.

6. Under the **Plane Orientation** section, select **Reverse Plane Normal**.

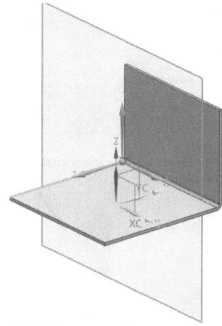

7. Click **OK**.

8. Draw the sketch, as shown.

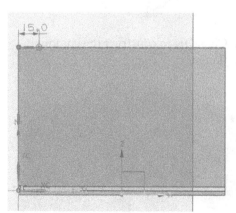

9. Click **Finish**.

10. On the **Contour Flange** dialog, under the **Width** section, select **Width Option > To End**.

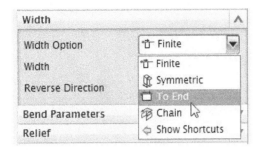

11. Double-click on the arrow attached to the sketch.

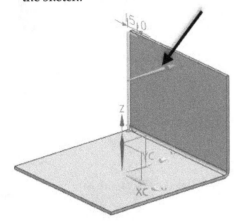

12. Click **OK** to construct the contour flange.

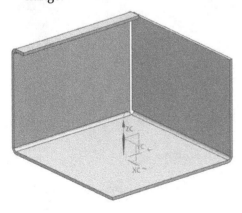

Adding the Closed Corner

1. To add the closed corner, click **Home > Corner > Closed Corner**.

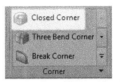

2. Select the two bends forming the corner.

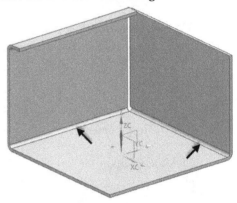

3. On the **Closed Corner** dialog, under the **Corner Properties** section, select **Treatment > Open**.

4. Click **OK** to add the open corner.

You can also apply corner treatment using the options in the **Treatments** drop-down. The different types of the corner treatments are:

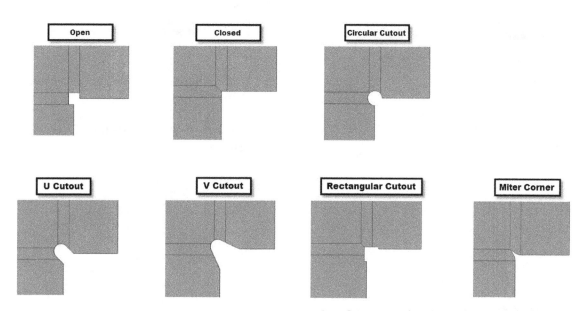

Adding the Louver

1. To add the louver, click **Home > Punch > Louver** on the ribbon.

2. Select the front face of the flange.

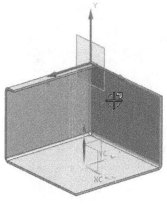

3. Construct the sketch, as shown in figure.

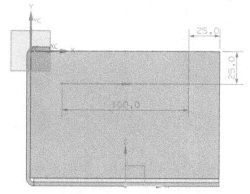

4. Click **Finish**.

5. On the **Louver** dialog, select **Louver Shape > Formed**.

6. Type-in **5** in the **Depth** box and click the **Reverse Direction** icon below it.

7. Type-in **10** in the **Length** box and click the **Reverse Direction** icon below it.

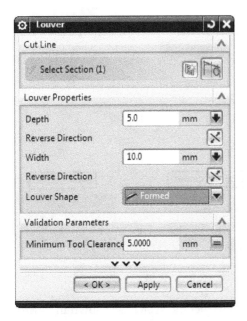

8. Click **OK** to add the louver.

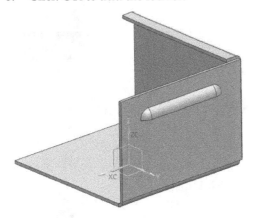

Making the Pattern Along curve

1. On the ribbon, click **Home > Feature > Pattern Feature**.

2. Select the louver feature.

3. On the **Louver** dialog, under **Pattern**

Definition section, select **Layout > Along**.

4. Under **Direction 1** section, click **Select Path**.

5. Select the vertical edge of the flange feature.

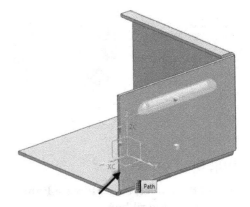

6. Under the **Direction 1** section, select **Spacing > Count and Span**.

7. Set **Count** to 3.

8. Set % **Span By** as 60.

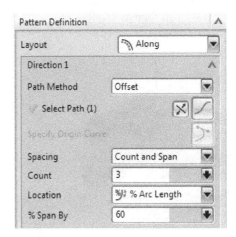

9. Click **OK** to construct the pattern along curve.

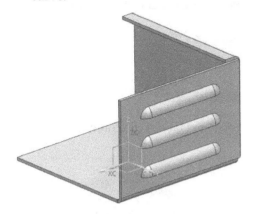

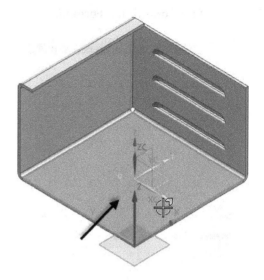

Adding the Bead

1. To add the bead, click **Home > Punch > Bead** on the ribbon.

2. Select the top face of the tab feature.

3. Draw a line and dimension it.

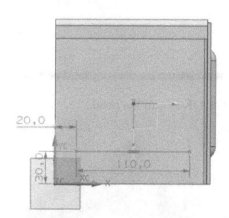

4. Click **Finish** on the ribbon.

5. Under the **Bead Properties** section, select **Cross Section > Circular**.

6. Set **Depth** to 4 and click the **Reverse Direction** icon below it

7. Set **Radius** to 4.

8. Select **End Condition > Formed**.

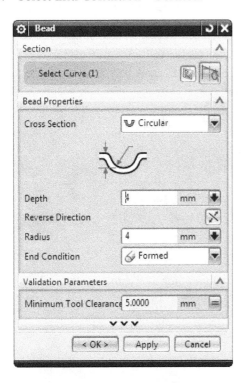

9. Click **OK** to add the bead.

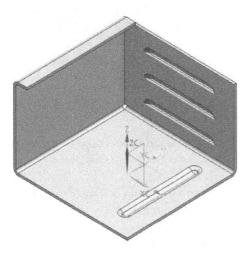

Adding the Drawn Cutout

1. To add the drawn cutout, click **Home > Punch > Drawn Cutout** on the ribbon.

2. Select the face of the contour flange.

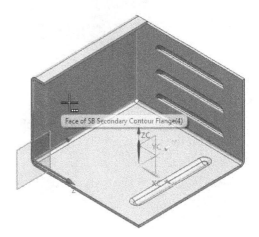

3. Draw a circle and dimension it.

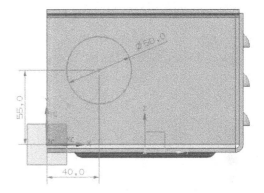

4. Click **Finish** on the ribbon.

5. Set **Depth** to 10.

6. Set **Side Angle** to 5.

7. Select **Side Walls > Material Outside**.

8. Expand the **Drawn Cutout** dialog.

9. Under the **Rounding** section, uncheck the **Round Section Corners** option.

10. Set **Die Radius** to 3.

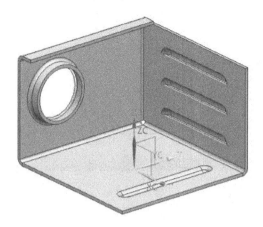

11. Click **OK** to add the drawn cutout.

Adding Gussets

1. To add gussets, click **Home > Punch > Gusset** on the ribbon.

2. Click on the bend face of the contour flange.

3. On the **Gusset** dialog, select **Type > Automatic Profile**.

4. Under the **Gusset Placement** section, select **Placement Type > Fit**.

5. Set **Count** to 3.

6. Under the **Parameters** section, set **Depth** to 12.

7. Select **Shape > Round**.

8. Set **Width** to 10.

9. Set **Side Angle** to 2.

10. Set **Punch Radius** and **Die Radius** to 2.

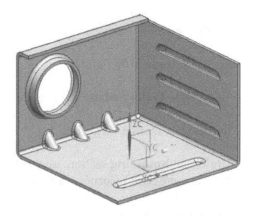

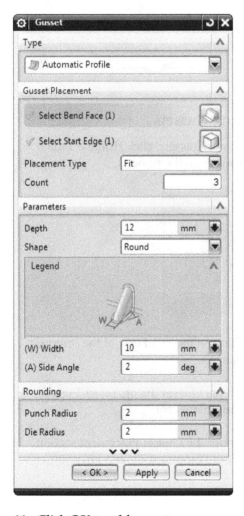

Constructing the Mirror Feature

1. To construct the mirror feature, click **Home > Feature > More > Mirror Feature** on the ribbon.

2. Under the **Part Navigator**, press the Ctrl key, and then select the contour flange, closed corner, bead feature, and gusset.

11. Click **OK** to add gussets.

NX 9 Tutorial

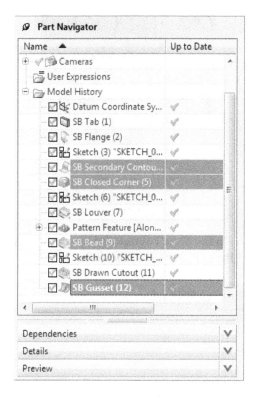

3. Under the **Mirror Plane** section, click **Select Plane**.

4. Select the YZ plane.

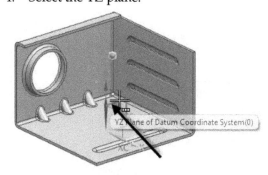

5. Click **OK** to construct the mirror feature.

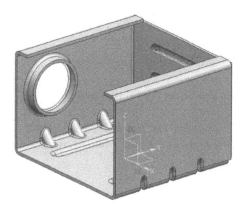

Making the Flat Pattern

1. To make the flat pattern, click **Home > Flat Pattern > Flat Pattern** on the ribbon.

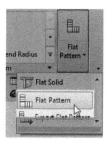

2. Click on the top face of the tab feature.

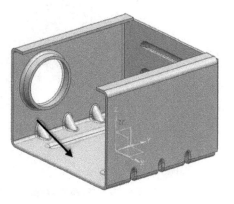

3. Uncheck the **Move to Absolute CSYS** option.

4. Click **OK** to make the flat pattern.

5. On the **Sheet Metal** message, click **OK**.

6. To view the flat pattern, click **View > Orientation > More > New Layout** on the ribbon.

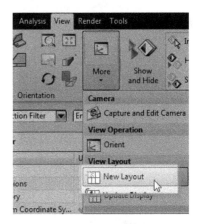

7. On the **New Layout** dialog, select FLAT-PATTERN#1 and click **OK**.

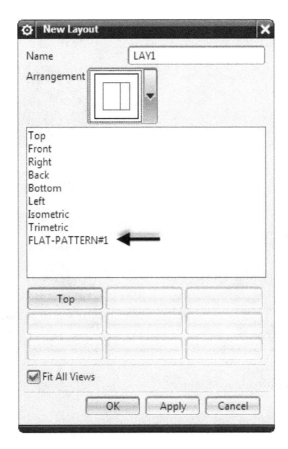

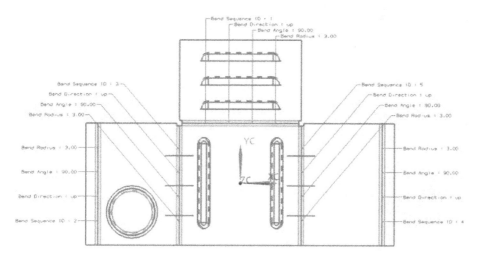

8. To view the 3D model, click **View > Orientation > More > New Layout** on the ribbon.

9. On the **New Layout** dialog, select **Isometric** and click **OK**.

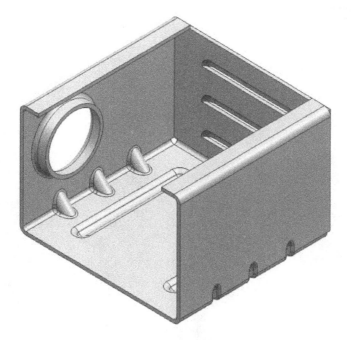

10. Save and close the file.

www.ingramcontent.com/pod-product-compliance
Lightning Source LLC
Chambersburg PA
CBHW080427060326
40689CB00019B/4413